SO-AKN-326

Elite Tennis
A Guide

Svetoslav S Elenkov

© 2017 Svetoslav S Elenkov. All rights reserved. No portion of this book may be reproduced, stored in a retrieval system, or transmitted in any form or by any means—electronic, mechanical, photocopy, recording, scanning, or other—except for brief quotations in critical reviews or articles, without the prior written permission of the author and publisher.
ISBN: 1543080014
ISBN 13: 9781543080018

Table of Contents

Introduction and Outline

ELITE TENNIS IS a book written as a guide and inspiration to those seeking to achieve greatness in the sport of tennis. It's comprised of the most important lessons, tips, and perspective that a player needs if they are to achieve the highest level of tennis, or simply to unleash their personal potential best.

The book assumes a considerable starting knowledge of the game of tennis. Although the writings are not geared toward beginners, I believe that anyone can gain great insight into the sport by reading this book. Within the text, there are scattered quotes by individuals like Miyamoto Musashi, who I've found to be the most influential competitor and writer in my life. The last chapter will explain more on this topic.

re, every time. Sometimes I cry, pout, and pull in pro-
st. To this day, I don't know how I managed to attend the
mber of classes I did.

At age 8, my dad comes to one of my practices and sees
hat virtually no progress has been made. He decides to
ake matters into his own hands and gets more personally
nvolved with my development. The schedule intensifies
to more than just a day or two a week. He and my mother
spend some time observing private lessons by tennis pros
who teach other students (a cheap alternative to tennis
education), and my dad and I try to apply some of the principles into my game.

After a few months, I'm ready to try my first tournament. I have 3+ years of "training" and am ready to destroy
my competition. However, I lose 8-0 in a pro-set to a
9-year-old kid. I think the only point I get is a double fault
from my opponent.

Without a doubt, I could have won the match! I think to
myself. I curl up into a ball in the middle of the court and
start crying in disbelief. The match belonged to me, but I
did not win. I do not believe the outcome. It is an impossible moment.

I could have won. I should have won. I can win. I wanna
play him again!" I say to my father (in Bulgarian) after I
calm down a bit.

"No, you couldn't have. The kid was too good," my dad
says.

It is not a deadly blow, but a motivator. I saw what level
I had to reach first hand, and now I'm about to do it. We

About Me

"**YOU ARE SO** lucky to be born with such talent." now I hear this from time to time, and though I reply w thank you, I resent the comment, and it turns my ston inside out. Only if they knew.

To understand my journey, you will have to take a t with me back in time to the very beginning.

At age 5, my parents decide that I have too many phys cal ticks and sport would be good for my development. There are two choices when it comes to sport in Bulgaria in the year 1989—tennis and soccer. Being the hooligan sport of the time, soccer is out of the question, which leaves them with tennis. I am to become a tennis player.

After my first experience in a group class, I quickly fig- ure out that I can't bounce the ball more than twice in a row or do any of the cool stuff that the older kids can. I am not physically gifted and just about as athletic as your average 5-year-old kid, if not less.

I struggle to come to practice. I'm dragged, baited, begged, and reasoned with by my Grandmother to get me intensify our practice schedule. I practice more seriously. I'm more focused and determined about my play. We enter more tournaments which have similar results, but I am not swayed. I can see progress, and it motivates me even further.

I become 9 years old, and I score my first tournament match win after a year of constant losing. After school, I run 2 kilometers to practice almost every time, and I run again on the way back. When I get home, I play soccer with the neighboring kids until the sun goes down. My dad writes my teachers to excuse me from school so we can attend more tournaments during class time. I love the process as it lets me skip the dreadful classroom time. To this day, I remember the disapproving face of my teacher as she tells me, "Another tournament huh? Good luck!"

By the time I hit 10 years old, I'm battling for the top 10 spots in the nation (of Bulgaria), and I win my first 200 bucks from placing #1 in my city's open tournament for juniors. At age 11, I'm already in the top 8 nationally after my first tournament in the 12 and under division. My parents find a ran-down volleyball facility which is not used for anything and is owned by the city. They talk their way into using the courts and build a tennis facility. The people in charge are OK with it, because at least the space is used for something instead of being a dump.

My grandfather gets involved. My family reads how to build clay tennis courts, measures up the space, divides it up, finds an investor, purchases the materials, and just builds the courts. We now have our own training facility.

Yes, it is robbed on the daily by local thieves, but no matter. It is a home base. I am now to represent my own tennis club (club tennis is a big deal in Europe).

At age 13, my family and I move to the USA with a strike of luck. We come with very little resources, which means all 4 of us must work (my sister, dad, mom, and I). I don't earn much as I'm very young at this point and am not expected to contribute to the bills. But tennis takes a back seat anyway.

The local clubs are not of high enough standard, and I lose inspiration. By age 15, I lose the desire to play. I still go to practice but uninspired and confused. I suffer from a self-diagnosed identity crisis, and I enter my "dark years." The dark years means little to no quality tennis from age 15–22.

At age 22, I finally finish a 2-year community college degree which takes me 4 years to complete. I'm about to transfer to a big university when I have a revelation that I don't want to do that. School has never brought me any joy or positive experiences. Why continue? Instead, I decide to focus on tennis. That is what my intuition is telling me. I do not have a plan or a goal. I just know tennis is what I need to do.

I play and train every day. I find hitting partners. I play against the wall. I read, learn, watch, and soak up everything that is tennis. I teach on the side and focus more on understanding the game. I improve—fast.

I find consistent hitting partners and devise a schedule. I follow my program, and I enjoy it. I've pursued tennis for the better part of my life, and I find that it is what makes me happiest. I throw myself in the local adult Open tournaments. By 23, I already have experience playing abroad into the professional circuit. I come back from tour, and figure out what I need to do to improve my performance. I conclude that I should not have quit between ages 15–21. Great. But that doesn't help. I decide that I need to practice more. I go "crazy mode." I work out more often, hit more often. I drink, eat, breathe, and dream tennis. I do nothing else.

At 10:15 p.m. during a practice match, I hit a topspin serve. I feel a sharp pain in my lower back. The serve is in, so I keep playing. I get a backhand which I swing with full force. I feel my back give out. It's as if someone stabbed me with a screwdriver in my lower spine. I fall to the ground—unable to feel my body. I think I'm paralyzed. I get scared. I don't know what to do. After 15 seconds of eternity, I finally roll on my side and attempt to get up. Tingling feelings mixed with sharp pains make this process difficult for me. It is the first match I retire from in my entire life. I don't know it at the time, but it is also the last match I would play in my competitive form and spirit.

My tennis playing career comes to a sudden end. Now, don't feel sorry for me. Yes, I did spend 3 years in denial about my circumstance. I saw 9 different doctors and chiropractors. Yes, I was misdiagnosed for a few months and treatments made my injury worse. And yes, I eventually came to terms with the fact that I was never going to play competitively again. But it's OK. I learned what I wanted to learn. I played with some of the best tennis players in the world, including a few in the top 100. I experienced what I wanted to experience. I achieved my goal and dream from when I was a little kid—to become the best tennis player that I can be. My chronic injury also gave me the chance to refocus on learning the tennis game even further and dive into the tennis teaching profession, where I have received much satisfaction helping others further their tennis goals. I've helped adults make the transition from 2.5 to 4.0 rating in a year. I've helped kids who had never played before become #1 ranked in their age division in Northern California. I've also helped kids become very good D1 tennis players and Pros.

Now that you know my story, we can start. If you want to become a great tennis player and avoid my mistakes, do yourself a favor and listen to my advice. I've spent most of my life exploring what it takes to be successful in tennis, and I think it would be unwise to avoid what I have to say.

There is a saying translated from Bulgarian to mean "Don't ask an old man; ask an experienced man."

1
How Do You Become A Great Tennis Player?

"All men are the same except for their belief in their own selves, regardless of what others may think of them."

—MM

THE QUESTION IS very straight forward, but the definition of "great tennis player" differs from person to person. Everyone needs to figure out for themselves what that definition is. And this is step one. For some, it could mean playing for their college team. For some, "great tennis player" could mean winning playoffs in their 3.0 NTRP USTA league. For some, it could mean becoming the #1 tennis player in the world.

I will tell you how to achieve these goals. Yes, I know how, and yes, I will tell you. Let's start with the most ambitious goal of all, and then you can scale it back so you can understand the price you must pay to achieve these goals. You must do as much of what I say as your life allows in order to achieve your goals.

Yes, there is a price to pay for all of this. The payment may include money, time, stress, and most importantly sacrifice. The sacrifice does not become apparent until you are faced with it. For most, the sacrifice may be unthinkably big and a price too high to pay. The sacrifice may come in the form of a ruined relationship with your friend, coach, parent, significant other, or all of them. The sacrifice may come in the form of decreased lifestyle or missed opportunity or the elimination of choice in life paths you planned on taking. The sacrifice may come in the form of financial risk or mental and physical health. The sacrifice may be your life's future.

It is the sacrifice that pushes hopeful tennis players off their path. It is that price that only very few pay to be the best or even one of the best in the world.

Now, it's time to explore all that is important and relevant in becoming a great tennis player. To achieve the highest of goals, you must fulfill all of this, as everyone who has been great in tennis has, and there are no shortcuts.

2
The Principles

The younger, the better

I USED TO try to figure out if there is an optimal age for starting a sport. But I've become convinced that this age is 0. After reading enough and having plenty of teaching experience, I can tell for certain that the kids who start the youngest do better with tennis. As a parent, if you are planning on having a champion tennis player, then start as early as possible. Have your kid play with balls and toys as early as you can. It'll be good for their physical and mental development anyways, even if you decide to veer off the tennis path later. Having developed some motor skills early will improve their chances of successful development greatly.

I've had a 5-year-old student who caught 0 out of 30 balls from a 2-foot toss right into their open hands. Yes, that kid still has hope. I'm the last person to tell you anything is unachievable, but it will be that much harder if you start sport later in life. Physical awareness is extremely important for the development of an athlete, and there is a good reason to start early.

Having said that, it does not mean that starting tennis older eliminates the possibility for great success. I know of a professional tennis player who started playing at age 14. This is a very rare occurrence. If you want to become a pro, you are 14 years or older, and have not had any tennis, I wish you luck. Just know the odds are stacked against you, and you will have the hardest journey in the history of tennis pros. Maybe you can use that as motivation. Refer to my comment about sacrifice.

Learning the learning process
As young or as early as anyone can grasp it, an under-standing of the learning process should be established. Technique must be learned; awareness has to be discov-ered. An athlete must learn to have concentrated con-trol over their body. An athlete must learn to feel their muscles contracting and activating in succession to cre-ate fluid motions. An athlete must learn to locally control their muscle groups to do specific tasks, and instill them into their "auto-pilot" mode, or subconscious memory through repetition.

Training the subconscious memory of your body is the key to the physical learning process. An athlete needs to learn to communicate with their body and have a good and healthy relationship with it. There needs to be an acceptance of failure, and a quick re-concentration and refocus to the task at hand. An athlete needs to be able to disassociate and associate different muscle groups with each other to learn technique effectively.

The awareness process may take a long time to develop, but it's important to teach it to yourself or others first. Unfortunately, rarely does anyone do this first, because it doesn't really put you in the action right away. So, what does this entail? The awareness process is the ability to match up what you think is happening with what is really happening.

There are many ways to improve this skill of awareness. One way is what I call the "reality check." You can use video or a mirror and see if you can attempt a motion and then match it to what really happened. Be precise. If there is no camera or mirror around, you can close your eyes and perform a motion, then open your eyes and check if the motion ends up at the exact location that you imagined it ending up. A simple example is extending your arm to your side horizontally to the ground and giving a very elaborate "thumbs down." Open your eyes and check if the thumb is pointing exactly down. Is your arm straight? Is your back as straight as you thought it would be? Is your head straight? Where is your face pointing when you open your eyes? How many degrees off 90 are you with your hand? Is your shoulder or forearm rolled? Is your right side a bit hunched over?

You can do this right now. Stand up and try it! Ask yourself these questions. This is a way to improve your physical awareness. See if you can disassociate the back roll with your shoulder roll and forearm roll. You may feel a weird and awkward feeling as you try to do that. This is a great sign!

Learning the learning process - the language of the body

The weird feeling that you get when performing something new is a signal from your body. This signal is part of a whole language you must learn if you want to be able to communicate with your body. Your body is trying to tell you something. In this case, the weird feeling is your body's way of telling you that you are attempting something new. This does not mean that the new thing is a good thing or a bad thing. It just means that it's new.

Another signal, or form communication, the body uses is pain. Pain when performing a motion means interference. The motion performed is interfering with something that your body structure doesn't agree with and does not accept at this time. This is most often a sign that the motion is not bio-mechanically correct. The less common scenario is that there is something wrong with your body. In either case, your body doesn't accept the motion at that time. It's important that we determine the difference between weirdness and pain.

The body has other "words" it uses to communicate with you. Recall the physiological responses to nervousness!

Nervousness means uncertainty, and often lack of preparation. It's your body telling you that it doesn't believe the outcome of your future activity is certain and doesn't believe that you will be OK at the end of the activity. In this case, more mental and physical preparation, or experience is needed. The lack of preparation can come in many forms; from not having enough practice to having arrived at your match 5 minutes prior and are struggling to get your things in order. Your body will be in shock from the new environment. Nervousness from lack of preparation could also manifest itself simply from not having had enough or having too much breakfast. It's difficult to pinpoint the source of nervousness, but it must be done. The good news is that finding the reason for why you are nervous is a skill, and this skill can be improved.

All body signals take priority when it comes to performance. This is really worth repeating. All body signals take priority when it comes to performance. If you have to go to the bathroom, you will not perform to your fullest. If you are hungry, your body is telling you that it needs fuel to function. If you are thirsty, obviously, you haven't done your homework and hydrated properly. Your body will prioritize its needs before it can perform to its fullest. If you are tired, likewise you haven't planned or trained for performance. Jet lag or sickness, likewise, can have a big impact on performance. These are not excuses; they are facts. Deal with the facts, and don't use them as excuses!

There are other ways the body communicates. Language can even come in the form of feel. When you swing your racquet and the ball lands away from the

center of the strings, you feel a slight jolt. This jolt is information that you need to interpret. This jolt lets you know
that there is a difference between where you aimed to
swing and where you actually swung. You can adjust your
motion based on the feedback you are getting from your
hand and arm, or shoulder. I call this process calibration.
You can improve efficiency by noticing how tight certain
muscles are. There are many ways to listen to your body,
and you need to learn as many as you can to improve to
your fullest potential.

Now that you understand how the body communicates with you, it's time to speak back. Fluid communication between you and your body muscles will improve not
only your performance but your calibration from day to
day and shot to shot. It will also improve the rate at which
you learn new physical motions and concepts.

While trying to master the 2-way communication with
your body, there are many common beliefs as to how to
achieve that which should be avoided.

**Ways of communication with your body that don't
work include but are not limited to:**

1. Hitting yourself. Don't do it. Don't slap yourself
or hit yourself on the head or anywhere else with your
racquet or your hand when you make a mistake. The
body interprets violence as a command to be passive
or erratic. Usually, that's the opposite of what you are
trying to achieve by slapping your hip or punching your
strings. The body will just continually shut down until

you let it play again. Imagine what happens if you keep hitting an animal. It will retreat to a corner and put its tail (if it has one) between its legs and twitch every time you raise your arm or whatever you use to hit it. In some instances, it might lash out in desperation. The body acts the same way. This will not improve your performance. Stop hitting yourself!

2. Talking to yourself. What's funny is, I was going to write a book called "Your body doesn't speak English." This is true. You cannot communicate with words to your body. Stop doing it! You need to speak its language. Animals read your tone and body language much more than vocal words. Your body responds in a similar way. Altering body language and attitude will communicate much more to the body than actual words.

3. Emotional outburst, or apathy. Acting out or conversely refusing to participate just distorts your attitude toward your task at hand and your performance dips. Your body will take your lead and lose focus. If this is not what you want to communicate, don't do it! Save the emotional outbursts for after you finish your match or after your lesson or training session ends, if you have to. Be emotionally stable. Try to channel emotional energy in a way to improve speed or gain focus when playing. A simple example is releasing excess energy on a first serve, running superfast for a drop shot, or simply executing a deeper splitstep. If low on energy, you can take your time and observe what is happening in the match. Use the time in between points to come up with a strategy. You may even give your body a chance to rest when you do that. Find a way to stay emotionally stable. If you are a high-energy person, then stay high energy during the whole match, like McEnroe. If you are a low energy person, then find a way to stay low energy the whole time, like Sampras or Murray.

4. Melody. This may be a bit controversial, but I believe that music does not help you gain tennis rhythm, and does not help you calm your nerves. You need to discover and address the source of nervousness instead. You can listen to music before or after your tennis session, but tennis rhythm is different from musical rhythm. The time it takes for the ball to reach your strings is different every single time, while a beat in a song is constant. To play tennis well, you need to alter the timing of each individual shot based on many factors, including positioning, conditions, strategy, ability, etc. It's better to find a flow of the game that works based on real-time events rather than a conjured song.

5. Other people talking. If your body doesn't listen to your own words, imagine what kind of a distraction other people are. If you can comprehend other people's words while translating those words into physical motions, then more power to you. Though this is very difficult and I don't recommend you do this outside of a controlled setting. I've personally struggled with this and seen others struggle. It's especially important when training a kid. They don't have that capability. If you want to explain something to a kid, simplify it and say it in between practice shots, or in between practice sessions and matches. Or even better, grab their arms and do it for them if they are too young. When I say simplify, I mean simplify. If you are a parent or a coach, try crunching your whole 30-minute feedback speech into one sentence. The less talking, the better. This also may be controversial, and very hard to implement in the tennis teaching profession, but I believe that a few down-to-the-point sentences are much more valuable than prolonged speeches and constant verbal motivation, or a series of "Great shot!" comments. You must be the primary communicator to your body. Other people can be a big distraction.

Learning the learning process - moving
This may seem strange. You know how to move, right? Think again.

From the moment I first laid flat on the tennis court after my back breaking incident, I knew something had gone terribly wrong. My concerns were confirmed 6 months later when the MRI came in showing a blown disc and 2 others about to do the same ... But that wasn't enough for me. I had to find out just exactly why this happened. the many months of therapy, I was fortunate enough to meet many different experts on rehabilitation who had an excellent grasp on the mechanics of the body. They inspired me to look further into how the body should be moving in congruence with its muscle and bone struc-ture. The findings were interesting and enlightening. **Here** are just a few core principles that I took away from the whole experience:

1. Every motion (at least in tennis) either starts or goes through your lower spine. It doesn't matter if you are hitting forehands, backhands, overheads, or volleys; your motion has to start or go through your lower back. Where the hips meet your back is the powerhouse of your body, and it is severely underutilized in the West, and some Asian cultures as well. From when we are young, we are taught how to sit on chairs for hours and hours on end. Sitting puts little to no strain on the muscles in charge of keeping your spine straight and in place. This means that the very muscles that initiate virtually every motion in tennis are not strong. As a result, we usually bypass them. We make up the lack of strength by using other, more developed muscles—even to walk. This brings me to my next point.

2. Walk from heel to toe. Don't "stand on your toes." While running, of course, your heel will not touch the ground, but your foot will still be rolling from heel to toe. You do not want to look like a ballerina (I have nothing against ballerinas; I like ballet!) and put your toes down first when moving around the tennis court. Pay attention to what part of your foot lands on the ground first when you begin to move, especially when turning. You may be surprised. When we utilize the heel to toe movement, we engage muscle groups that are usually neglected, and weak. Get used to it, and strengthen these muscles!

3. The kinetic wave. Or the kinetic chain, as some people call it. Every motion you make draws energy from a previous motion. It is important to move by activating muscle groups in succession in a smooth manner. You shouldn't strike a ball with your hand before the whole body has contributed to this strike.

The principle of the kinetic wave works by employing the law of conservation of energy. Suppose we float a tennis racquet in the space station, and after a while, it hits an object at the bottom of the grip, the top of the racquet will now have roughly doubled its speed. It will rotate around its center mass about twice as fast relative to the space station and any objects sitting at rest in the space station. This is how energy will transfer through your body each time a joint like the hip, shoulder, or elbow "hits the breaks" and lets the rest of the body or arm continue to move. This isn't an easy thing to master. However, once you have enough awareness of your muscles, you should make large strides in mastering this area. Build on the momentum your body has already generated! Employ muscles actively in stopping larger and slower rotations in favor of smaller and quicker ones as you go up the kinetic chain toward your point of contact.

One great way to make sure you move smoothly and in succession is to keep the muscles in charge of your next motion loose until the absolute last moment before they are needed. Muscles act as an On and Off switch. If your bicep is already activated, you can't "activate it even more." The muscles that are in charge of your shot the most need to be off prior to their time of need. This can be confusing, because you obviously need some muscles activated in order to get to the ball and position yourself well. This is where body awareness comes in. Your muscles are going to contract the hardest and perform the best at the moment of activation. When they stay active, they become fatigued and weaken their performance rapidly, even if in your mind they are working just as hard as moments ago.

Now that you know about the learning process, we can move onto our next principle.

Discipline and Consistency

> "[Do not] allow your heart to be swayed along a side-track."

> —MM

If becoming the tennis player of your dreams is your goal, then you must schedule for it! It has to be a priority, and not an afterthought. If work is getting in the way, schedule your work around it. If school is getting in the way, schedule school around it. Yes, move your schooling schedule to make way for tennis. You want to be great, right? Being great at something is not a hobby or an afterthought. You must be serious about your progress. The more you stick to your schedule, the quicker and more substantial progress you will make.

There are more than a few reasons to always stick to plan. You need to adhere to your practice schedule rain or shine (I'm not suggesting playing on wet courts), energetic or not, inspired or not. The quality of your training sessions matter, too. But at the very least, if you are not getting anything productive out of your tennis session, you are still training yourself to always show up and to stick to a schedule. This will become a very important skill if that one big match happens to be on a day that you just ... don't feel like playing.

Having a strict schedule will also allow you to track how much you are playing and practicing, and it will give you a sense of how much more or less you need to do. Try to relate the amount of practice to your progress, sustainability, physical and mental health, and then increase, decrease, or reschedule accordingly. Having the numbers of what you have accomplished so far will also hopefully give you more motivational fuel to keep going.

Now, let's talk about how much you need to practice and what.

What should your practice schedule look like?

"Even a thousand-mile road is walked one step at a time. It is the duty of a warrior to study this art without hurry, and practice it over the years. Try to defeat today what you were yesterday, defeat lesser men tomorrow, and stronger men the day after."

—MM

I believe practicing 1 hour a day per week is better than practicing 7 hours only on Sundays. I believe that practicing 2 hours per day is better than practicing 4 hours every other day. And finally, I believe that practicing 2 times for 2 hours a day is better than practicing 4 hours at once every day.

And this is your number. 2 sessions of 2 hours of training totaling in 4 hours a day is how much time you will need to invest to be a great player. Obviously, this number is going to be different for every person, and may or may not be sustainable, but the breaking up of sessions is important to regurgitate information and experience. If tennis training is just a hobby for you, then you may only practice once or twice a week, and squeeze in a league match or a tournament whenever you can. But the discipline needs to be there in order to progress. You need to have allocated time specifically for tennis practice. I heard a quote the other day: "If you ain't improvin', you are gettin' worse." I'm not sayin' it's true. But I'm sayin' it. See what I'm sayin'?

On top of the ~4 hours a day, I believe it's important to read books and watch video regularly about sport, competition, and physical activities, as well as continuously exploring new ways to improve the quality of your practice.

Be aware that training more than your body can handle carries physical risks, which will not help you progress, but set you back. Not only will your body lack the time to recover, but may lead to overuse injuries. This is what happened to me.

Personal story time. When I came back to the States from playing some tournaments in Australia, I decided to pick up my practice frequency. I just wasn't good enough, I thought. I looked at the person who has probably hit the most tennis balls in the world—Andre Agassi. If he could do 1,000,000 per year, or ~2,740 a day, I could double it.

I decided to hit 5,000 a day, and I did. I had practice matches, feeding sessions, and ball machine time scheduled. I was pulling 4 baskets or 1,000 balls per hour + a match or rally drills. The training was intense and exhausting. I loved it. I was seeing the ball as large as a watermelon when I stepped on the court, and it seemed like it was traveling slower than a container ship powered by a cooling fan. My timing was impeccable. I even lifted weights at the end of the day to break down my muscles even further (not saying this is the right thing to do; more on this later). I'm not gonna lie; at the end of the week, I felt like the best tennis player in the world. I happen to play someone who had some ATP points at the time and destroyed him in a series of 11-point games. I don't know what would have happened if we played a match. But I tell you, I felt unstoppable! Until, of course, I popped a disk in my back. And now I'm not playing tennis anymore. Lesson learned! Personal story finished.

The point is, you need to find a schedule that works, and is challenging, but not dangerous. I would experiment and play around with the time you spend on and off the court training, and then focus on quality. You can train for longer than 4 hours a day, but make sure your body can take it, and you are recovering and replenishing.

If starting out at a young age, I recommend shorter sessions for the kids. I think 30–45 minute intervals are enough to keep them attentive. Perhaps twice a day for 30 minutes would do the trick and get them in the habit of a scheduled day. Once more mentally and physically capable, this period can be enlarged and intensified. This process will be different for each kid.

If you are really crazy and won't settle for being second best, you can try for 3 training sessions per day. Wake up. Drink (water or sports drinks!). Eat. Practice for an hour and a half. Drink. Eat. Practice for an hour and a half. Drink. Eat. Play a match. Drink or eat something with protein. Read or watch some videos. Sleep. Repeat.

What to practice
Now that we figured out tennis needs to be your life when it comes to time devotion, we need to talk about what to practice.

Not all practice is equal. If you spend 4 hours a day talking about how cool your Nike shoes are and how your friend from school totally sucks at tennis, then you aren't really practicing. If you are spending most of your time on the bench "hydrating" or "discussing" your game score over the middle of the net, then you are not practicing. If your phone isn't on silent and in your bag (unless it's being used productively for video or tracking, etc.), you are not fully practicing. Make sure you are deliberate and serious about your progress, because your progress will be just as serious as you are.

So, what exactly should you be practicing?

"You can only fight the way you practice."

—MM

I'm glad you finally asked. The answer is this: you get good at what you practice. Mind-blowing, right? Well, let's break it down a bit. If you want to be good at striking a ball, you can practice striking balls, and you will improve. If you want to be good at hitting forehands with good technique, you need to practice hitting forehands with good technique. If you want to be good at hitting proper forehands in a rally, then you practice that. If you want to hit proper forehands within a match, then you need to practice your forehand during a match. If you want to be good at playing tournament matches, you need to play tournament matches.

Ok, this answer is true, but it sounds like a bit of a cop out. I agree. Here is what your priority list should be when practicing:

Fundamentals. I don't do Martial Arts, but someone told me that their Taekwondo instructor says getting a black belt really comes down to the mastery of just 7 moves. Tennis isn't that much different. There are 7 different striking motions that require mastery: the overhead motion, forehand, backhand, forehand volley, backhand volley, forehand slice, and backhand slice. That's it.

These 7 shots should take priority in your practice session. It should be the first thing you do and get out of the way when you step on the tennis court. The ratio of which shots you should practice more can vary, depending on the playstyle you plan in mind. If you like going to the net, then volleys and overhead/serve motion should make up most of your fundamentals workout. If you like to play from the baseline, then ground strokes should be your focus.

A very successful 30-minute practice session can look like this:

Ground Strokes
20 forehands down the line. 20 backhands down the line. 20 forehands crosscourt. 20 backhands crosscourt. 20 wide forehands crosscourt. 20 wide backhands crosscourt. 20 shots alternating forehand and backhand cross court. 20 shots alternating wide forehand and backhand shots. 20 short put-away forehands and backhands.

Short break, then volleys
20 forehand volleys down the line. 20 backhand volleys down the line. 20 forehand volleys crosscourt, then 20

backhand crosscourt. 20 high floaty volleys where you move in to hit it on the forehand side, then 20 on the backhand side. 20 low dig volleys on the forehand side, then 20 on the backhand side. 20 shots alternating forehand and backhand random volleys. 20 overhead/volley alternating shots. 10 bouncing overheads (letting the ball bounce before hitting it), 10 retreating scissor-kick overheads.

Short break, then approach shots
10 '5-shot' combinations. The '5-shot' combination looks like this: a crosscourt groundstroke, followed by a topspin or a slice down the line approach shot, 2 volleys and an overhead. You can simplify this drill to be more focused on approach shots, but it will be a ton of running compared to time hitting balls.

Short break, then 20 serves on each side
If you are efficient, you can fit all this in 30 minutes. It's an ambitious goal, but possible. Yes, you will need at least a ball machine or a very good ball feeder on the other side who has accurate feeds and can keep pace with your ability. If none of this is possible, then you will have to be creative on the wall. I spent a ton of time practicing on the wall to cut costs, and it is possible to get much of your work done there. You can practice every one of the 7 strokes on the wall, including the overheads (hit the ball in such a way that it bounces prior to hitting the wall. This will cause it to pop up for your next overhead). The other

option is a hitting partner, but the fundamental work will not really happen—as the incoming ball needs to be accurate—and you are going to spend your time hitting most of your shots away from our optimal strike zone and at a random sequence if partner is not super accurate.

The breaking up of different shots will keep the fundamentals fresh, and the completion of the numbers will give motivation and a sense of progress. The fundamental work is also quantifiable and should be logged so it can help you judge your program later. The numbers can be changed. If you are ambitious, you can do 30 shots or 40 shots per exercise. Although you can, you don't need to spend more than 30 minutes on fundamentals a day in my opinion. If there is one thing you should do every day, it's this.

The rest of your practice time can consist of rally drills and matches. I suggest spending no more than 5 minutes per specific rally drill. Use a timer, or have your parent, coach, or friend time you. Parents often love helping their children during practice, so overseeing the clock will be a very useful and harmless way to be involved in the on-court development of a player.

Side note time! Unless they are an expert at the sport, I should add: I do not encourage much parental feedback about a child's tennis. A tennis parent's role is support and general guidance. Chances are that the child understands more about the game than the parent, even if the kid can't articulate it. It's OK to share your thoughts with your child, but it needs to be in the form of a discussion and questions—not instructions. Instructions which don't match up with the child's vision for their game will be resented and ultimately may cause the destruction of the tennis dream, and possibly the relationship in the family. In this case, instruction leads to destruction. More on this topic later. Side note over!

Rally drills can fill up at least another 30 minutes, or they can be substituted by learning different variations of fundamental shots. For example, short angle topspin crosscourt shots, lobs, drop shots, drives or half volleys can all be used as substitutes. Practicing 1 or 2 different variations of fundamentals per day may help keep things fresh and interesting for a tennis player. Each person will be different as to how much variety they need in their training.

After the rally drills, you should practice some point play. Make sure that the point play is very constructive. Think about the points and the way they play out. Try to find trends and study them. See if you can pick up on a shot that you would like to learn and practice after your fundamentals the next day. Also, experiment and try to be aware of situations or limitations that you experience during play so that they can be addressed the next day.

After your point play is done, your 1 and a half to 2-hour session is finished. That was quick, right? The second session can be a repeat of the first session, or a match, or both. Make sure you refer to my comment about knowing how much your body can take. Also, I suggest entering tournaments or more official events to get an idea of how your progress is coming along and what you can do to improve further.

Ok, so now you know about what you should practice. But are you doing it right?

Quality is undoubtedly a very big component of your path to success. This is why many people pay ridiculous amounts of money for professional tennis training and instruction. It's very valuable. Having a high-quality coach can make a big difference. The market for coaching is very tough, and on top of that, every coach will come to you with their own perspective on things they believe are important. Regardless, you really need to have someone to teach you and check up on your fundamentals every now and then (at least weekly). Of course, it helps to have a coach with you all the time, and teach you the different variations of the fundamental shots and more. How much quality coaching you receive is going to bring us back to the conversation of sacrifice. Is it possible to make it big without a coach? Yes. Again, the challenge is enormous, and your body communication should better be an A+ if you are going to learn tennis from watching videos on the internet. It's important to keep in mind that the world of tennis is based on competition. The ones with the highest quality training, the largest amount, and the most concentrated training will climb to the top. You need to out-edge and out-work everyone else.

Edge, you ask? One topic you should be discussing with your coach is what you have that nobody else has. This one thing is your edge. What was Sampras' edge? The serve. What about Nadal? Physique, endurance, and mental strength. Federer's edge? Hair. But really, it's his technique and mental endurance. What about Djokovic? Flexibility, passion, speed, resolve. Ask yourself what your edge is. How are you going to defeat your opponents? What type of mini-game within the match do you want to beat them at?

Side note time! I don't want to bash internet content on tennis, as there is a small fraction that is very useful, so I'm going to try to take it easy. However, online instructional videos are not a very good way to learn the basics, as they can be interpreted differently by people, and are almost always out of context from your perspective. For example, a video may try to teach you the open stance, but the video doesn't know that 100% of your forehands are slices. Is the video wrong? Perhaps not. Does it apply to you? No. Should you seek professional help with your tennis? Yes. Side note done.

Where to practice
Some believe that one must practice in the hottest, most humid places on the planet with the most resources. Namely Florida. No one can argue that many successful tennis players come from such environment. Are the results a product of climate, or the resources and the

resolve of the individuals? Some argue and swear by high-altitude training, and some believe in training at the beach where the ball becomes a slush of water and salt by the second set.

In my opinion, you need to train in the environment you plan to play matches in. If you want to be a clay specialist, go to Spain, train with them, and win the French. If you want to be a great indoor carpet surface serve and volleyer, then practice indoors in the perfect still-air and dim lighting conditions. If you want to excel in hot conditions, go practice in hot places. If you want to be versatile, then relocate your training cycles so that you can have experience with everything. It's as simple as that.

Technique - Hard rules

> *"A straight road is made by leveling the earth and hardening gravel."*

> *—MM*

Tennis technique evolves with time as technology changes and the rules are altered. At the year I'm writing this, I can tell you what you need to set you on the path of good technique. **These are just very general rules and can be molded. It is important to keep that in mind**.

1. Use continental grip for every shot, except for your groundstrokes. This rule has been in play for a very long time, and I don't think it's about to change anytime soon. The continental grip provides a very stable access to both sides of the racquet in a very short period of time and is perfect for maximizing overhead motion pronation. If you are using anything other than continental grip for your shots, then you don't have great technique. You could be doing things better. Does a professional player hopeful need to switch to a continental grip tomorrow? Yes. Does a weekend warrior casual player need to switch to a continental grip tomorrow? The decision depends on how much time and match performance they are willing to sacrifice to learn it. This is a personal decision.

2. Keep your back (and head) straight. Don't bend it sideways or backwards or forwards. I don't care when and who says what. If you need to bend over a bit, do it from your hips. Don't curve your back. If you need to lean back to hit a topspin serve, bend from your knees. Don't bend your back backwards! If you need to do a "bow curve" on your serve, don't do a "bow curve" on your serve. Keep your back straight! Yes, rotating while using your spine as an axis is perfectly fine and encouraged, but bending it is not. Don't do it! With other shots, if you need to get lower, take a bigger step so your distance between your legs is greater, lunge, and hinge from your hips. Body bends are for emergency shots only, and not encouraged at all. It is important to note that by body bend, I basically mean spine bending to the left, right, forward or back. Twisting is another matter and is encouraged.

3. Turn your body. There needs to be a unit turn prior to every shot in tennis. It should be the first thing that happens when preparing to hit a shot, and it needs to happen every time. If you are not clear on what a unit turn is, you can look it up, but it's a roughly ~90-degree rotation of your upper body, depending on the type, location, and goal of the shot. The hips, legs, and core provide power for this turn, and it is enabled by a heel-to-toe rolling of your outside foot, and a heel-to-toe step with your inside foot.

4. Don't lock your joints. Your elbows and knees should never be locked and 100% straight. Once the first ball is hit, that's it. The only time the elbow can and should be locked is during the toss on your serve.

5. Hold your racquet at the bottom of the grip with your main hand. There is a slight exception to this if you hold your stick with both hands on the forehand side as well as the backhand side—then you can be a bit more adventurous. But for the love of tennis, don't go to the other extreme and hold too far down so your pinky or even ring finger is hanging off below the end of the grip! The stability and blocking power transfer you will gain by having all of your hand on the grip will far outweigh the extra "snap" you think you are getting on your swing.

6. Master control before power. Increase the power of your shots very gradually. If at any point you feel like you are missing more than you should, you probably took a big leap in attempted power output. In a match, there is usually 1 or 2 shots that I'd hit with 100% power, and those shots are usually serves or the occasional raging forehand.

"To wield the long sword well, you must wield it calmly."

—MM

To produce more power, you must exaggerate your preparation and swing, as well as enforce continuity. Continuity means that your stroke does not have periods of decreasing or stagnating speed. The speed of the racquet should be at constant acceleration. To sum it up—create power by enlarging and smoothing your stroke. Your strength will determine how fast your racquet will accelerate. There are 10-year-old girls that hit with 80 MPH or more. It's possible to hit a very heavy ball without much strength. Also, remember to keep your mistake ratio in check as you are trying to empower your game. Only hit as fast as you can control.

7. Always run, walk, or cross-over step towards the ball. Never sidestep or back pedal. Sidesteps and back peddling should only be used for recovery purposes. Sidesteps and back pedals are the slowest movements available to us and are the most dangerous to employ. You should not be in a huge hurry when sidestepping or back peddling. When approaching shots that are not far from you, I recommend a unit turn, followed by a heavy walk (lowered body, heel-to-toe action) or cross-over steps (also mostly heel-to-toe action). The cross-over steps can be done in many directions which will eliminate the need for back peddling. If you are not agile enough to do cross-over steps, work on your agility. When approaching shots that are far away from you, I recommend running, followed by a slowdown prior to impact.

8. Focus of your vision should be on the ball. When positioning for a shot, always keep the focus of your eyes on the ball. You can absorb information with your peripheral vision, but do not lose focus of the ball even for a second (except maybe if it is against the bright sun; avoid the sun!). Keep your eyes focused on the ball even when running for a lob. Never turn the opposite way after hitting a shot. Keep your eyes focused on the ball even after you hit your shot, not just prior to impact. In other words, this means that your head should always be facing in the general direction of the ball.

9. After every shot, you should attempt to recover to the appropriate recovery point. The full system of recovery spots is too complex to put in writing; however, it can be described as the midpoint between the opponent's 2 best shots on either of your sides (and maybe a 3rd over your head). In addition, unless you are making an educated guess about a highly offensive incoming shot, you should split-step every time the opponent is about to strike the ball, even if you have not fully reached your recovery point. If you are very advanced, you can work your split-step into your recovery sidesteps and crossover steps.

These are some rules that you should remember when taking lessons, watching videos, or just trying to alter your technique. If what you are trying to do contradicts these rules, then it's probably not the best thing for your game. Stay within the rules as much as you can!

Technique - Controversial issues
1. What stance should I use? Silly question. You need to master all stances, and, in fact, you should be using hybrid stances, depending on the shot. Virtually any stance you can think of between closed, neutral, open, and all their nuances should be used in tennis. There is a time and place for almost any leg position. Moreover, don't worry so much about your stance. You need to focus not on stance, but on unlocking your body with your legs and allowing it to perform the function you are going for.

Not only are different stances appropriate at different times, but their viability also varies, depending on how the player is holding the racquet. The more aggressive (towards western grip—on the groundstrokes) the grip, the more favorable open stances will be to that player. If the grip is more conservative (towards a continental grip—on the ground strokes), then the neutral and closed stances will not only feel better—they will be more effective most of the time.

Ok, this is very broad. Can I give you some examples of what you should be doing and when? Yes, sure!

Let's say you're either lucky or studious, and you've managed to develop a forehand grip that lays somewhere between a semi-western and an eastern grip. In this case, you should be stepping into shots toward a neutral stance on most attacking shots like a drive down the line, or a bouncing overhead. If you are counterpunching on the baseline, you should most likely be using open stances on your wide shots. If you are approaching with a backhand slice, then you should have more of a closed stance and perhaps do a crossover step after. Let's say you are handling a high ball far behind the baseline. In this case, your stance will most likely be somewhere between open and neutral stance.

But what exactly are these stances, you ask? A neutral stance is a leg position that forms a straight line involving your right heel, left heel, and your target. An open stance is a leg formation where your driving leg is on the outside and forms a perpendicular line to your target with your non-driving leg. A closed stance is the same as an open stance, except the position of your legs is reversed.

2. Should you loop on your forehand? What about your backhand? Absolutely, but don't go crazy. The racquet should be taken back no further than head height level, and even lower on your backhand. The reason why looping is better than not looping is the loop's versatility. You can always drop your racquet head lower as you are going for your strike, but you can't always bring it higher. You will notice that people who don't have loops on their strokes have a hard time driving the ball flat, have trouble generating enough power for their efforts, and their shots are always predictably topspin. I encourage everyone to learn how to hit with topspin, slice, and flat.

3. Pinpoint vs. classical stance on the serve? Sure. Use them both, or choose your favorite. I haven't seen anything to lead me to believe one way is better than the other. The viability of the stance may even vary, depending on the player's physique and balance.

4. How hard should you grip the racquet? I believe in efficiency, and I think the racquet should be held just tight enough to keep good form during the preparation, and gradually gripped harder up until impact. You should be holding your racquet the tightest during your hitting zone.

5. Should you jump on your serve? Sure. Just know that jumping on the serve is a result of good technique and not the cause of it. You may be jumping at the wrong time, or using the jump for the wrong reasons, like to gain height on your serve. That is not the function of the jump. The real reason why the jump exists may surprise you. The jump on the serve allows a player to turn their body frictionless in the air. That's it.

6. Should you slide on the court? Sure. But know that the slide is a result of good technique combined with the strive for efficiency and stability. If you are sliding just because someone else is doing it, then you should not be sliding.

7. Should you have a big backswing, or should you shorten it? Silly question. You need to be able to do both. Always plan for a big swing, but be ready to cut it short at any moment. The length of your swing should depend on how much time you have to prepare, and what you plan on doing with your shot.

8. Should you exhale on contact? Breathing patterns for tennis players and all athletes in general is a much-debated topic. There is a school of thought that teaches exhaling during strikes. This technique is presented as a way to improve timing, as the alignment of the breath and stroke could reveal a discrepancy in timing and serve as a "reality check" of when events are happening and how far off your prediction you are. Another benefit of the exhaling technique is that it encourages breathing. This may be comical, but there are many tennis players who hold their breaths for very long periods of time and become winded by the end of each point. Not breathing is very detrimental to your efficiency. Your body does not get the oxygen it needs, and you become very fatigued.

My suspicion, however, is that no player who has devoted their life to tennis will ever suffer from breathing problems. It is impossible to play for hours without regulating your breathing. I've tried various breathing techniques and experimented over the course of training sessions. I believe that consciously controlled breathing takes away from the body's natural strive for efficiency. Perhaps it's possible to train your body to breathe in a specific pattern, so it does not require consciousness, but even then, I believe that the body would have come up with better ways to breathe on its own given enough time.

I believe you should breathe in practice and matches the same way as you breathe normally when you walk, run, or sleep. You should let your body take a breath whenever it needs without restriction. I believe that breathing, being a semi-unconscious process, can be left to the body to regulate, just as your heartbeat.

I've found that familiar breathing tendencies give me a more even surface upon which I can find better timing. However, I'm only sharing what works best for me. This issue, in my mind, is still a topic for debate when it comes to other tennis players.

9. Should you stare at the contact point? Good question. I've personally looked at pictures and slow motion video of most of the top 100 players in the world to answer the question of what they do. I've found that only about 20% look at the contact point directly on the vast majority of their shots when striking the ball (Federer being one of the 20%). Most of the players, however, fix their sight in a position where their peripheral vision can see both the contact point and their target. I personally fall under that 80%.

I've tried playing while staring at the contact point for a while, and the results were negative. I felt like there wasn't a big difference in my % of miss-hits. However, I felt like I had much less vision of the other side of the court, and my accuracy decreased, as well as my court sense.

The answer to whether you should stare at the contact point or not is undetermined and subjective. I can't say for certain that if Federer were to look at his contact point with his peripheral vision instead, he would be an even better player. Also, I can't say for certain that Djokovic would be a better player if he were to stare at the contact point directly on every shot. This decision seems to be very personal and subjective.

10. Should you warm up with short court or mini-tennis? No. I actually have nothing against short court tennis. I do it regularly, but I just find better results and a quicker calibration process when the warm-up is started at full-court from the baseline. I find it's more efficient to transition from full-court to short-court play with accuracy than the other way around. I highly approve of short-court tennis for practice, especially when there is a goal. Some goals can include cross-court dip practice rally or slice-only gameplay within the service boxes. These exercises and games can be very fun, and productive.

11. 10-and-under tennis, and colored balls. I like the idea of making tennis easier to grasp for little kids. I think that various tools like softer balls, smaller nets, and smaller racquets are helpful in getting little kids to have more fun and be engaged in tennis. However, once a kid is athletic enough, and a decision is made to take the sport more seriously, I believe the kid should wield a racquet and ball as close to the official size as they can handle while performing good technique.

If a kid is fortunate enough to receive a controlled feed or hand toss, I believe that even regular size standard balls can be just as good, if not better, for the development of a young kid who is just starting out. The faster ball will challenge them more, and even though their failure rate may be very high, their eye will be trained to keep track of fast objects. This issue is up for debate. Personally, I oppose any rules and regulation forcing competition or training with specific equipment or court size (other than the official rules of tennis for adults) as every kid's development will be different. This decision should be left to the parents and the coaches. I should also add that I oppose any rules on the tournament side as well, which cripples the ability of directors and organizers to erect an event based on their liking and preference.

12. Symmetry vs. Asymmetry in tennis. This topic of what a tennis player should aim for is widely debated, and I'm afraid I can't lean one way or the other with my opinion. On one side, many physical trainers preach symmetric training and its benefits for health and injury prevention. On the other side, when we look at Federer's right forearm compared to his left, or Nadal's left bicep compared to his right, it's hard to say that asymmetry doesn't play in role in the specialization and eventual success of a tennis player.

It is likely that the best tennis players train symmetrically, and the pure amount of tennis they play specializes their muscle groups to deal with their specific playstyles and challenges. I have not met or heard of anyone who trains their muscle groups asymmetrically for tennis, so it's hard to comment on the effects. But what I can comment on is that there are some tennis players who do not do much physical training at all, except the heavy time they spend on the tennis court, and their bodies seem to be just as prone to injury as those who try to keep their body more symmetric.

There are arguments that having a symmetric body will carry extra unused muscle mass, and make you more inefficient as a result. There is also an argument that uneven muscle group development will lead to more injury and an early playing retirement. It is unknown to what extent bone structure evolves with the asymmetric development of a tennis player. Considering current trends, I would advise not to be experimental, and follow the prevalent symmetric physical training. If there is conclusive evidence in the future which supports performance increase with minimal risk from asymmetric training, then this decision can be re-evaluated. As with any other big decision, make sure it applies to you, and it's not just a general suggestion.

13. Timing. I believe humans are terrible at timing short real-time events. Striking the ball is a short real time event. The ball spends somewhere between 1/100th–1/50th of a second on touching the tennis strings. It is impossible for you to time the ball as to strike it in this exact period of time. Most of your shots should be focused on having a long "hitting zone." A hitting zone is a period during your stroke in which you hope to contact the ball. The more uncertain you are about the exact contact, the longer the hitting zone must be.

A large hitting zone is obvious in shots like the volleys. The volleys spend close to 100% of their motion facing your target (or the appropriate angle to hit your target). Likewise, a groundstroke should spend a considerable fraction (maybe 10–50%) of the stroke in a hitting zone. Wristy and whipping motions spend very little time in a hitting zone, and therefore have very mixed results, including many shanks and unpleasant weak shots or loose racquets. This is one reason why the error rate for swinging volleys of all kinds is high.

14. Technology and equipment. I'm all for it. Any advance in technology which helps you improve should be utilized if possible. Of course, you should be aware of the cost vs. benefit factor before making decisions about the latest tech gadget or software. As far as equipment goes, I think that the highest quality possible is always advisable. If you cannot afford the highest quality racquet, shoes, or clothes, you are only making your life harder relative to your competition. Find the funds! Don't skimp on racquet cost. Playing with sub-par racquets will cost you much more in the very long run.

15. Switching racquets. "Switching" is always a hurdle, and it should not be overlooked. If better technology is available, you should take advantage of it. Yes, you may have to undergo a period of adjustment, but the reward will be worth it. You should not be afraid of change. After all, your most valuable quality should be adaptability. If you can't even adapt to a new racquet, you need to look at completely re-evaluating your priorities and mindset. Yes, I know Sampras and Federer used the same racquet for most of their career, but that doesn't mean they couldn't have done better with a newer version of their loved instrument. Djokovic underwent a switch or two, and he didn't seem to have a problem climbing to #1 in the world. Over-familiarity can be a weakness. Focus on adapting rather than familiarizing.

16. Should you use a 2-handed backhand or 1-handed backhand? Try both, and choose your favorite. Chances are you will be happier playing with whichever feels best for you. Both have their advantages and disadvantages.

2-handed backhands are great for absorbing and blocking power. This property is especially important for return of serves. Returns are the second most important shot after the serve, and the 2-handed backhand will give you a great advantage here. The disadvantage is that the stroke is limited in size and motion. The reach is not very good, and the versatility lacks. Most tennis players use 2-handed backhands now, and the benefits arguably outweigh the deficits.

1-handed backhands are more versatile. 1-handers can generate larger swings and in theory produce more powerful shots. Looking at players like Gasquet and Wawrinka, it's hard to dismiss this theory. The disadvantage of the 1-hander is the lack of blocking power, which results in a generally weak return. The preparation for a 1-hander is usually more elaborate, and the unit turn is difficult to execute in high-speed rallies. Because of its inferior stability, the 1-hander also lacks performance in the case of a miss-hit. Timing your 1-hander does not allow for much margin for error.

Even though there is somewhat of a consensus that 2-handers are generally better because of their ability to withstand power more effectively, there are plenty of success stories for 1-handed players. I feel like the choice between the 2 comes down to personal preference and the choice will not weigh heavily in your result.

17. What is the best forehand grip? Semi-western. It matters more what your game's objective is, what your skill set already is, and what surface you mainly plan on playing, etc. If you land anywhere between the semi-western and eastern forehand grip, I think you are in good shape. The best grip isn't universal to everyone. Some will do better with specific grips depending on comfort. Furthermore, some will do better with different grips depending on playstyle and surface.

Personal story time! I switched very late to an eastern grip from a semi-western grip. One might think I was crazy, but I did it for good reasons that had to do with my own personal style, plan, and the mentality of my own game. This was a very specific decision. My choice came down to my inability to execute an offensive pressure game with my higher contact point, and favorably lateral footwork related to my semi-western grip. Also, my strokes were too geared for topspin shots, and my flat-shot production was suffering a bit. I needed more torque to hit the ball harder. Most of the players I was playing were getting to

every single one of my "winners." I had to be more asser-
tive. A shot from inside the court had to be a winner, and
a flatter shot is a good way to go. I achieved the results I
wanted through much practice, and even to this day, I train
others in drills using my eastern grip. It's a versatile grip,
and I'm able to produce much power on command with it.
Personal story done!

Strategy

> "To become the enemy, see yourself as the enemy
> of the enemy."

—MM

Strategy should be something you think about well after
you've had plenty of match experience and are ready to
really play the "game" of tennis. It's very hard to focus on
where, when, and how to hit the ball if you don't have all
your shots on auto-pilot. You need to have some mastery
of your shots before you start paying more attention to
the other side of the court rather than your own.

Strategy: Shot Selection

Until you are well practiced, there are a few general guide-
lines that can help you through a tennis match. Let's start
with the singles strategy. It's called hitting the ball crosscourt. Most of your groundstrokes should be crosscourt,

and for good reasons. For one, you don't have to change the direction of the ball. By hitting the serve back crosscourt, you are hitting the ball in the direction it came from, and this shot requires less timing perfection than a down-the-line strike. Hitting crosscourt also allows you to hit over the lowest part of the net, and it gives you a few feet extra length to hit into. The biggest bonus of hitting a crosscourt shot is that your recovery point is very close to you. After a crosscourt shot, you need to side step just a little toward the middle to hit your optimal recovery position. Hitting down the line opens up the court to your opponent, and you are going to struggle to cover it.

That's it. That's all you need to know. Ok just kidding ... kind of. Here are some other tips.

Once the point starts, your goal should be to look for an opportunity to draw a short ball, a mistake, or score a winner, depending on what your style is, but you must hit the right shot at the right time. You should not be hitting winners or approach shots from 5 feet behind the baseline, and you cannot be scoring lobs from 5 feet away from the net. Likewise, you should not be hitting drop volleys from the service line and deep volleys from 2 feet away from the net. Every shot has its time and place. Intelligent shot selection is a big part of being successful with your strategy.

You should only hit down the line for one of 3 reasons: the clear majority of your approach shots should be down the line, most of your finishing drives(winners) should be down the line, and all your direction change shots should be down the line.

What is a direction change shot? Well, let's say you are getting killed on the forehand to forehand rally, and you want to change the dynamic of the exchange. To do that, you are going to have to pull off a direction change. You are going to have to hit a down the line shot from a ball that's coming at you at an angle. That's a direction change shot. It should not be fast—a direction change shot should have some topspin and be generally loopy. The reason for this is that you will need to cover the court after a shot like that, and you will need to travel further to reach your recovery point.

When should you slice the ball? What's the deal with this shot? Slices are a specialty tool that can be very fun and effective. **There are 4 main different types of slices:**

1. The Knife - a fast, heavy backspin shot typically hit from above the net, which sometimes has a downward trajectory. Once the ball contacts the ground, it skids and stays very low. If one were to observe the shape of the shot, it looks almost like a straight line, which probably contributed to its nickname.

2. The Chop - a power absorbing, fast, downward chopping backspin shot designed to kill pace and land short (around the service line). The Chop's goal is to bring the opponent off the baseline and force them to dig the ball from a low position. The chop does not bounce high, and it aims to have the ball bounce a second time very quickly after the first—forcing the opponent to react and run quickly.

3. The Drive - an elegant stroke typically hit from the baseline which sails low over the net and bounces deep into the court (preventing the opponent from attacking it). The Drive has a bigger swing than most of the slices and does not aim to put much spin on the ball. Instead, the shot transfers most of its energy to generate depth by swinging in a more horizontal way than the rest of the slice family.

4. The Drop - a shot that can be performed from anywhere on the court. The Drop Shot is a stroke that requires high amounts of touch, and its goal is to bounce as close to the net, and furthest away from the opponent as possible. Drop shots typically have high amounts of backspin, and almost no drive.

That's it. The knife, the chop, the drive, and the drop. Yes, they rhyme.

That's all nice and dandy, but I haven't answered when you should hit these shots. **Here are some situations where slices are applicable:**

1. Approach shot. The slice is well-suited as an approach shot. The ball stays short, so you will not be in big danger of the lob, and it stays low, so you will not be attacked by a blood-thirsty opponent trying to score some skin. If they try to smash the ball with 100 mph, geometry dictates that the ball will either hit the net or go out. All you must do is get out of the way, and you will win the point in this case. Types of slices best suited for approach shots: chops, knives.

2. Change-up shot.

"Learn the rhythm of your opponent, and use rhythm that your opponent doesn't expect. You win by creating formless rhythm out of the rhythm of the Void (more on this later)."

—MM

A change-up shot is simply a shot that changes up the rhythm and dynamic of the rally. A direction switch could be considered a change-up shot. Slices are effective at changing the direction of the rally, because they are slow! A slow shot will allow you enough time to recover to the appropriate position on the court. The slice hopefully stays low and does not set your opponent for too much offense. Types of slices best suited for change-up shots: drives.

3. Winners. Yes, you can hit winners with a slice. The backspin family has something good going for them. The ball tends to bounce quickly after its first bounce. (Yes, I know why this happens, but this is not a physics book, so I will not explain why!) This fact makes it harder for your opponent to get to the ball in time. Types of slices best suited for winners: drop shots, knives.

4. Emergency shots. If you are in a full sprint to get to a ball you can barely get your racquet on, then slice usually ends up as the only option. If your arm is stretched out and you are diving or doing the splits as you are striking the ball, you will most likely end up with an emergency slice. This type of shot usually aims at keeping you in the point. Typically, this shot is hit very high over the net as to buy enough time for you to recover. Hitting the ball short, low, or slow will usually allow the opponent to close in and finish the point off. Types of slices best suited for emergency shots: N/A.

5. High balls. In some cases, it may be a good idea to handle the very high bouncing balls with a slice. If your backhand is not very trained up high, then it becomes a viable option. Just remember that if you don't want to pop the ball up, your slice must always strike from above the ball. Types of slices best suited for high balls: drives, knives.

How much topspin should you put in your shot? Silly question. It varies, of course. The topspin amount is determined by many different factors. The more time you have to set up for your shots, the more topspin you can hit (doesn't mean you should; more topspin is not always better). The floatier the ball, the more topspin opportunity you have. However, how much topspin your shots ultimately have is determined by other variables like:

1. What are you trying to do with the ball for each individual shot? Are you lobbing, driving, pushing your opponent back, changing up the rally, drop-shotting, volleying, approaching, counter-punching, grinding, moonballing, or ...? Obviously, an offensive topspin lob will have much more top than a drive, for example.

2. What is the surface and ball condition? Are they suited for a lot of topspin? Your effort to hit with heavy topspin will not pay off on a fast, slick surface, for example. You will be wasting your energy. On the other hand, you could get very good results with heavy topspin on a slow clay court on a hot day at low altitude with heavy balls!

3. Does your opponent like topspin? How tall are they? What grip do they play with? For example, if your opponent is 6'10 and plays with a western grip, then the last thing you want to do is pop the ball up into their strike zone. However, if your opponent plays with a continental group and is 5'1, then topspin may come in handy.

4. How good are you at the topspin game? Will hitting with tons of topspin be effective for you? Do you enjoy it? The answers to these questions must be considered.

5. How fit are you? Topspin shots require a lot of energy. Are you as fit as a 19-year-old Nadal? Make sure you factor your fitness in your playstyle.

Answer some or all these questions, and it will become apparent how much topspin you should hit with in general, match to match, and how much you should hit with from shot to shot.

What about your serve? The goal of the serve is to put your opponent in disposition. You must serve the ball in such a way that it makes it hard or even impossible for your opponent to return it, and if they do, you don't want it to be a hard shot. To do this, you can get creative. This is one game you can play with your opponent even if your shot is not necessarily on auto-pilot. You have time to sit back and watch your opponent's returning position, their body language, and their grip. You have time to think about what kind of returns they have chosen in the past, and what their favorite stroke is, and how they move prior to your serve. You also have time to judge how fast they are and what you think they are expecting from you. After taking all of this into account, you can choose a serve out of your toolbox and see how it performs.

My tool box, you ask? Yes, I suggest learning all 3 (4, including American twist) types of serves: slice, flat, and topspin. After having a good grasp of each, you can combine a bit of each to form your own unique creations. Using a variety of serves is a great way to throw your opponent off timing and draw an error or a weak shot you can later pounce on.

The return? This one may be complicated. There is so much that goes into returning. It's much more important to get the return technically right, than where you place it. You need to decide what type of return you are mostly going to go for (offensive, or just get the ball in play), which will determine how far into or outside the court you will stand. Where to stand is the second most important thing. The third most important is where to place it. Placement doesn't really matter all that much, because in higher level, the serve usually dictates where the return goes, and it's not like you'll get a chance to think about it much when the ball is traveling towards you at 130 MPH. The return will be very instinctual. You can premeditate a bit, but it won't make much of a difference. If you do get a good look at the serve and have time to position properly, then what I suggest is you look to attack. Punish the server for giving a weak ball, and they will stop doing it, and start double faulting!

Strategy: Exploiting weakness

> *"It is difficult to move strong things by pushing directly, so you should injure the corners."*

> —MM

A common strategy to defeating an opponent is by exploiting a weakness. This works especially well if the opponent is very strong—even stronger and more skilled than you. If you can manage to find a weakness, or at the very least a shot they don't enjoy hitting, or a situation they don't like being in (like running for drop shots for example), then exploit it. Place the ball in the least comfortable place for them many times until they start yielding a weak shot, or change their way of playing (since plan B is usually worse than plan A, this means you are lowering their level of play). This is a way of beating even players who appear tougher than you.

Strategy: Shot matching

"There is appropriate time and place for the use of various weapons."

—MM

Another basic strategy is matching up your strengths with your opponent's weaknesses. This depends on how skilled and versatile you and your opponent are. Yes, we've all heard about the "hit to their backhand the whole match" strategy, but it goes much deeper than that. What if your opponent has a western forehand grip and hates low forehands? Why not play most shots with slices to his forehand side and see how they handle it? If you've got the skill, it's worth the shot. Play with your opponent and find out what they can't handle.

Personal story time! I was playing an AMT(Australian Money Tournament) in Australia once. On my first round, I happened to match up against the Romanian Davis Cup coach! It was fun, but he was in his 40's and clearly not in top playing shape. I won 6-0, 6-0. However, we started talking since our countries of birth border each other. We became friends!

The very next round, I got matched up against a big hitter who wiped me clean in the first set 6-2. My Romanian friend saw what was happening and did something against the rules. (Yes, I guess technically it's cheating, and I don't endorse it, but it's a fun story.) He called up his Bulgarian friend and asked him how to say "UP!" At the start of the second set, I took a glance at him, and I saw his index finger pointing up combined with the words "Nah Goreh!" This, of course, means "Up" in Bulgarian.

At first, the words perplexed me, but then I looked at my opponent and realized he was maybe 5 foot, 4 inches at the most. I took the hint, and started lobbing every single ball I could, and sliced the rest. I didn't give him any pace to work with at all! He just couldn't deal with the constant overheads from behind the baseline, and taking the ball out of the air failed. I can only imagine how frustrated he must have been. Anyway, I won 6-2, 6-2 in the next 2 sets to take the match. Personal story done!

Strategy: Style matching

> *"If the enemy thinks of the mountains, attack like the sea; and if [they] think of the sea, attack like the mountain"*

> — *MM*

Style matching means to change the tempo and the way you play against an opponent in order to be more effective. If your opponent is hitting the ball very hard, fast, and deep, do not try to out-hit them. Obviously, that's their best playstyle if they are adamant about using it and trying to impose it on you. Instead of trying to hit the ball faster than them, you must counter-block it, slice it, take some pace off, play from further behind the baseline, or simply redirect the shots. Do not play their game! The only time you should try to out-hit them is if that's your best playstyle also, and it happens to work better than theirs. In this case, they'll be forced to change, or they will lose.

Conversely, if a player is pushing and lobbing the ball, do not give into their playstyle; you must either start slicing, angling the ball, driving, or come to the net. Do not get stuck playing a back and forth game that lasts for hours, as that is obviously their strongest style. You must find a playstyle that is uncomfortable for them and force the match to be played on your terms.

Another example of this is dealing with "serve and volleyers." If someone is serving and volleying and they are being effective, you must take the ball early on the return. By doing so, you will not give them enough time to come to the net. The ball will catch them too early in their movement, and they will be ineffective. Another way to deal with this is by standing far back on the return and allowing the topspin serve (it will usually be topspin if they are any good) to spin for a longer period in the air, and lose its heaviness. Once the ball starts dropping down, you will have enough time to load up a shot and lob the serve and volleyer.

I will give one more example: If someone is hitting winners on your serve, it means that they are comfortable with what you are giving them. If you are already serving fast, then serving faster will not have a positive effect. You will just injure your shoulder, or start missing more. This is what they want you to do (subconsciously, or consciously). Instead, you must slice the ball, take some pace off, and make them move for the return. By not giving them much pace to work with, they will have to create all the energy of the shot themselves, on the run, and will not be such a big danger to you. Put them in disposition!

Strategy: In Conclusion
The larger point here is that strategy is important, but meaningless if you don't have the tools(skills) to execute it. This is something that can be discussed from match to match and learned through experience.

If all this thinking sounds too overwhelming or complex, don't be discouraged. It becomes automatic. You only have to think about your strokes and how to hit them for a period. After a while, your movements become automatic. Strategy is the same way. After playing enough matches, and discussing shot selection and matching, eventually, even this becomes instinctual. With enough experience and training, perhaps the only mental concern you'll have in a match is whether you like pink or purple more.

Doubles
Oh, man! I could probably write a whole book just on doubles strategy, but thankfully there are plenty of them out there, so I don't have to do it. Instead, I will tell you what

I think is important when playing doubles. It really comes down to 3 major things: positioning, skill, and chemistry.

I always tell the story of how John McEnroe won the SAP Open in doubles at age 48, with a partner who was 36 years old at the time. I was there and witnessed this happen in front of my eyes! Unbelievable! This event just drove the point home to me that speed, strength, endurance, and all the attributes that are usually associated with youth are not nearly as important as positioning, skills, and experience when playing doubles.

All 3 things important for good doubles play can be gained just through experience, except maybe your skills. The skills can be honed and practiced outside of match play, but the rest is really a product of many, many matches, and post-match analysis. It's tough to comment on positioning, because it's going to vary from team to team, and from individual to individual. A 5'1, 3.0 NTRP, 60-year-old lady is going to have much different positioning patterns than a 6'5, 20-year-old pro player. In general, I believe in applying pressure to your opponents as a team through movement and shot quality, playing per the flow of the point, and placing the ball in such a way as to not be attacked. I also believe in surprise, strategy, and learning through trial and error.

Fitness and diet
So,

You understand the learning process. You know how much to practice and what to practice. You know that you need a ton of match experience, and you know the importance of strategy and when its time and place is. But we haven't talked about fitness and diet yet!

"Is it really that important that we have to talk about it?" Yes. "Can't I just do a set of suicide lines per day and call it?" No. "But I just wanna eat cupcakes!" K.

Look, depending on how far in tennis you want to go, you must customize your diet and fitness schedule. Let's talk about fitness training first.

Fitness

Your physical training should be done before you start your tennis practices. You must already be tried by the time you hit the court. If you are already a decent player, you know how important it is to perform when you are tired. Why not practice playing tired—every day? I've done this, of course, and can tell you that after doing it for a few weeks, I am convinced it is the right way to do it. I used to work out at the end of my day, and that was not yielding nearly as much in terms of energy and performance.

Do land exercises. Don't go swimming for 2 hours a day and lie to yourself that you've done your training. I have nothing against swimmers and am not suggesting a swimmer is any less of an athlete. Swimming is just not suited for tennis training. The way muscles are trained to move, and use up energy is very different. The breathing is different, and the rhythm understanding is way off.

Don't run! Long distance running is bad for tennis players. Anyone who tells you to run a mile or 10 per day to get in shape for tennis should be fired on the spot! Also, stretch after exercise and training, not before. Stretching can improve range of motion if done right, but it can also harm you if done wrong. If you are confused or unsure of the right way to stretch, I will advise you to seek professional help. If you want to be the best, you must seek out the best to help you out. Usually, just one session with a high-quality trainer will be enough to learn how to stretch well.

The ultimate tennis training should take periodization into account. The tennis body will go through cycles to achieve peak performance. Many Pro athletes are aware of this and structure their physical training accordingly.

The peak performance cycle takes up anywhere from 3 to 6 months, and this is how it goes:

1. First 4–8 weeks is strength training. Before you start your tennis practice, go to the gym (or lift rocks and milk gallons!) and lift medium to high weight with high repetitions. I suggest hiring a trainer if you have the money and have them help you through this process. It's important that your lifting technique is proper to avoid injury and hit the correct muscles.

I suggest doing full body exercises which let you get done with your strength training in 45 minutes or less! You need time to rest and eat. You can't be spending all day in the gym looking at the mirror and taking selfies. You got things to do!

2. The second 4–8 weeks, you should be working on endurance. Pick your motions carefully and work on medium to high weight with high repetitions. This is the time where you post that 60 pull-ups in a row video or those push-up contests with your training buddy.

3. The final 4–8 weeks is plyometrics. If you want, you can wear a weight vest or ankle weights, but none of that is truly necessary. You need to work on jumping, switching directions, speed, and explosiveness. This is the period where those nifty direction change running drills come into play, and you litter your phone notes with your highest high-jump record. Let's see how many likes your tire-jumping slow-mo video gets!

At the end of the 3–6-month period, you are ready for your season. You can still do physical training, but only of the explosive variety, and very sparingly—maybe 2 times per week. Your performance will peak for about a month and then slowly start to diminish over time. You can pick and choose how many months you want to compete before it's time to have a break! Usually, 3 months is a solid period of performance. Then it's time for vacation! Go rest, take a break from tennis if you want, and live large knowing you've completed a cycle. In a couple of weeks, get started on strength training again to begin your second cycle. Do a few of these cycles, and you'll be the fittest player on tour (or in your college, or league).

Now that you know the type of training you need, all you have to do is find your favorite exercises that fit the mold, and you are set. I hope you enjoy your mornings! (I don't. I started at 10:30 a.m. I like to spend most of my morning in bed! With all of these time zones, it's 6 a.m. somewhere in the world, you know? Why do I have to obey Pacific Standard Time?!)

Diet

This is a tough one. I've tried the "carbo-loading" route, I've tried the "super low carb" route, and I've tried the "no grains" route. What I found works best for energy management is the "no grains" diet. I felt at about 4/10 energy level every day, and all day. Now, that may sound low, but I felt great. I could last all day with the same energy throughout the day with 0 energy crashes.

Having no energy dips is great, because the problem I experienced with the "carbo-loading" is that I'd have at 9/10 energy level for an hour and then start dropping. Also, with the carbs, I felt heavy, and sometimes I'd get dizzy in the beginning of my workouts. I'd have all kinds of energy fluctuations. I'd even have crashes all the way down to 0/10 and start getting depressed over the fact that I'm not #1 in the world, or that I have less money than Warren Buffet, and therefore life is not worth living, and my training is pointless. So, don't do that. This is pretty subjective, and I'm sure others may have different experiences. So, the most useful thing I can say here is seek professional help if you can afford it, and experiment with your diet until you find a balance that works.

Diet is important, and it's hard to detect its contribution in your performance. Having the wrong meal could mean the difference between winning 6-3, 6-3, to losing 6-3, 6-3. Don't underestimate it.

Becoming a super tennis player is becoming more than just a full-time job, huh?

Tournament preparation and environmental awareness

So, it's 9:55 a.m. and your match starts at 10:00 a.m. You grab your bag from the back of your car (or your parent's car) and rush to the tournament desk to check in. You are a bit stressed but think nothing of the situation. You step onto the court and feel like you forgot how to play tennis. Your timing is off. You can't aim the ball. You are confused and perplexed. You try to hit the ball harder because you know you can play so much better than you are playing right now, and none of your shots go in. You don't know if you should laugh or cry, so you do both at the same time. The match is over sooner than you can get a hold of your emotions, and now you have the longest ride back home, ever!

Sound familiar? If it doesn't, you either have super discipline or haven't had enough tournament experience!

If you have to travel more than an hour and a half for your tournament match, it's probably better to do it a day or two ahead, and stay at a hotel if you can afford it, or find someone who will room you. Traveling on the day of your match will throw your schedule off, especially if your match is early in the day.

The preparation starts the day before. You need to maintain regular eating schedule, but start drinking water the night before. You may have to go to the bathroom in the middle of the night, but it's worth it! If you do wake up, drink some more liquids and get back to bed! In the morning, wake up more than 2 hours ahead of your match, eat a nice breakfast, and continue to drink liquids. Your drinking should be in small amounts but over a long period. Getting used to waking up at a similar time as when you need to wake up for your matches is a good habit.

"Examine your environment."

—MM

Arrive at the destination of your match at least an hour and a half prior to start time. Look around and get familiar with the courts and the surroundings. Find out where the bathroom is. Find out where the tournament desk is. Find out if anyone you know is playing or will play at this tournament (this will avoid distractions and surprises later). Find out if there is a possibility to hit on the tournament courts, with the tournament balls. This is important, as you need to get acclimated to the new surface and balls. The surface and ball makes a very big difference, and you need to know what you are dealing with. As you are hitting, ask yourself how the ball reacts off the court. Does the ball slow down and pop up? Does the ball get fuzzy quick? Does the ball slide on the surface like a puppy with glass shoes on ice? All this information is extremely important and relative to your performance later on.

Now that you are adjusted to the courts you will be playing on, or at the very least studied how other people play on them, you are warmed up, and are ready to rest. Spend the next hour prior to match time eating very lightly and continuing to hydrate. Study other people playing and discuss your future opponent if you know who they are. If there are no chairs at the site, bring one. You need to be comfortable and resting from your 15–30-minute warm-up (which hopefully will include some point play).

Make sure that you bring not only a chair, but all the necessary supplies like a towel, plenty of liquids, and extra tennis gear in case of complications, including extra racquets, grips, practice balls, socks, outfit, and even shoes. If you want, you can bring a first aid kit, too! Look at the weather report and prepare accordingly. If you want to be a complete preparation boss, call the tournament director and ask them what the tournament ball will be, go to the store and buy a couple of cans for practice. Do not get caught unprepared! A wise tennis coach once said, "Failing to prepare is preparing to fail."

Your match is underway, and it's time to shine. The match, for the most part, is your chance to showcase how hard you've trained and how well you've prepared. Yes, the mind and strategy game within the match matters, but not nearly as much as your skill level and physical training. You can think of it as a stage performance. The more rehearsed you are for a performance or speech, the more fluid you will be, and the more you will enjoy it. You can draw the parallels to your tennis match. It's a great feeling to be toward the end of your second set, and just now decide to bring out your fastest serve. I want you to have that feeling! What I said about practice counts here. If you want to be able to play long 3-set matches, practice 3-set matches. If you want the ability to play 2 matches in one day, practice playing 2 matches in one day. You'll do great.

How should you treat your opponent? Treat them with dignity and respect. This topic is a bit subjective. Personally, I don't even want the win if I made a wrong call. I'd rather give the match away knowing it's undeserved. I always strive to make the right call. If someone challenges my call, I reassure them of my decision if I'm sure I saw what I saw. Make sure you state your decision loud and clear, so your opponent can clearly hear you. If they insist, I just give them the point and get ready for the next. To me, it's more important to control the emotional atmosphere of the match than to gain an extra point. By having control over the relationship between me and my opponent, I let the contest continue, which is a big thing if I'm winning. I give up a point, and they give up an opportunity to escalate the energy of the match. Seems like a good trade to me. If they are aggressively challenging the call, they are really looking to escalate as things are not going their way. Don't give them what they want. Of course, if they are continuously cheating, then you can seek out a third party to help with the calls if a referee is not already present. Like I said, this is what I do, and what I would do. Tennis match ethics is up for discussion and argument, but not if you are my student. I'm not advocating weakness. On the contrary, it takes much more mental strength not to be swayed by your opponent's emotional outbursts than to give into them and escalate along.

Once your match is done, you should already know when you play next and who. Go watch your opponent if they are playing and see if you can pick up anything useful about their game. Continue to drink small sips of your liquid of choice (hopefully water, a sports drink, or a combination of both) and actively recover. All the rest will fall in place. Tournament day should feel like celebration and fun, not stress. It's what you look forward to, and what you train for. Go talk to people, and joke with the tournament desk. Enjoy it.

3
Monetary Cost

HOW MUCH IS all this going to cost you? We talked about the many forms of payment for achieving your goals, including potentially enormous sacrifices. If becoming a top world class tennis player is your goal, then the costs are unthinkably great. Let's focus on monetary costs.

Typically, it would take you about 10 years +/- 5 to become a top pro following the 4-hour practice day and 45-minute physical conditioning for 6 or 7 days a week. If you want to relate it to Malcom's book, that's 7,300–21,900 hours of quality on-court time. If you want to relate it to Musashi's book, that's 1,825–5, 475 days to his 1,000–10,000 days. That's a large investment of time, money, and opportunity cost. Let's talk about a rough estimate to gain some perspective.

I recommend you meet with a private coach at least once a week. The coach should be experienced with the pro game, and know what they are talking about. Finding a great coach may be a big challenge. Anyway, depending on where you live, if you spend all your training hours with your private coach, that may total anywhere between $60–120 per hour (as of 2017). So, that would be a minimum of $60, and a maximum of $3,360 for private instruction.

If most of the time spent isn't with your instructor/ coach, but in a group clinic, you are looking at about $30–$50 per hour, making that total about $1,140 per week. If you are really strapped for cash, then you must find hitting partners and a very durable wall for a total of ~$15 a week for tennis balls.

You are a human being, and you will need to sleep and eat food. I assume you have support in that department, but if you don't, you can add the costs for rent and food into the equation. Depending on where you live and train, your costs may be large. Keep in mind that spending your time training will leave very little, if no time at all for working.

Equipment costs can run out of control. If you are getting powerful, you may be breaking a string per day. I would look for durable polyester strings to last through your training. The cost of strings will be anywhere between $10–$210 if you include stringing labor into the second number and break once every week instead of once a day. If you are training full time, you may not have time to string your own racquets. Racquet cost is not that much at first, but you'll need at least 3 racquets every 6 months later on. That's a minimum of 2 racquets per year for $400, to a maximum of 8 per year for a total of $1600 ($8–$30 per week). Shoes wear out quickly. You need to look for quality. At the peak of my training, I needed 1 pair of shoes per month. Quality shoes now are around $100–$150. At the minimum, you'll need $100 every 2 months, which is about $12 a week, or at the most $35 a week. Over grips are around $15 for 3, making it a $15 per week investment unless you want a new grip every day, which means $30. Clothes will run you about $100 a month, which makes it about $25 per week. Shock absorbers/dampeners are about $2; you need a total of 0, which rounds out to about $0 per week. Miscellaneous equipment (water bottles, electrolyte mix, towels, sunscreen, bug spray, etc.) ~$10 week. We are going to substitute tournament cost for a day of practicing for the sake of simplicity. There are other expenses like sports therapists and physical trainers, but we are going to count those out as they are not part of our schedule. My point here is that there are expenses that may add on additional cost, so be prepared.

Let's put some of these numbers together

For a quick learner with a ton of sport experience at age 10 and a small checkbook, the cost of being a top tennis Pro will be a minimum of $155 per week, $8,215 per year, or $41,075 for the minimum of 5 years. That's if you borrow someone's stringing machine for free, and possibly get a few pairs of shoes donated! This is as cheap as you can get, and you are working with a hungry (motivated), and very athletic child.

For a medium talent kid starting out at age 7.5, and factoring a 7.5 year progress timeline, the cost will be (this includes 7 private lessons a week at $90, 2 string jobs a week for a total of $80, $23 per week for racquets(6 per year), $30 per week for shoes(1 pair per month), $15 grips, $25 clothes per week, and $10 miscellaneous) a total of $813 per week, $42,276 per year, or $317,070 for the life of the investment (assuming, of course, that all costs stay the same, and please remember this is a rough estimate).

Finally, if you have an average kid, with little sport experience, at age 5, and you don't want to limit them in any way when it comes to time and quality, you may need 10 years to achieve your goal. This elaborate investment in the kid will run you a total of $3,685 per week, $191,620 per year, and $1,916,200 for the life of the investment.

To conclude, the monetary cost alone for developing a top world class tennis player is anywhere between $41,075–$1,916,200. I assume most people will fall into the $317,070+ range.

Let that sink in for a bit, but do not be discouraged. It only gets better from here. If you end up paying all that money, even if all else fails, the least you can get is 4 free years of education at almost any college with a tennis team you want. My former doubles partner Aaron Klapper pointed out that at $60,000 per year, it's almost worth it! The competition on the girl's side is even less, so with a smaller investment, college education is almost guaranteed. The investment may pay for itself right there.

Not only that, but the more successful a young and promising player is, the more noticed they get. The extra attention will bring in sponsors of all kinds. You may have tennis brands sending you free bags and racquets in the mail. You may get private individuals pitching in money for tournaments. If you look harder, you can even find plenty of people around the world willing to house traveling tennis players for free. On top of that, there are whole organizations that offer to train promising young tennis players for free. A "scholarship" of this kind may reduce the cost of training greatly. With effective management, the dream can be achieved for much less. To get the free stuff, however, the young individual must be noticed, and that means a very strict schedule for the first few years.

A side note about training programs! Scholarship-type programs usually afford to provide free training, because they use the talented individual to bring up the level of their program and their group classes. Inherently, there is nothing wrong with that. However, it is possible (but not certain) for the talent to be held back by the group. This isn't because the group is weaker in skill and ability, but because the group may rub off inferior work ethic. Also, there may be risks that come with the change of environment and system which may not agree with how you got to this level in the first place. So be careful! Side note ends here!

If you are older, I'm sorry to tell you, but there will be no one sponsoring you, unless it's a family member, friend, or someone who you manage to inspire. Most, if not all the cost will be paid by you. Also, all this cost doesn't consider the traveling expense for tournaments.

However, if you are doing things right, the winnings from tournaments at the end of your training program should offset the costs. If you work this much, with abandon, and unquestionable commitment, I don't see a way for you not to be able to make up your expenses through tournament play and sponsorships.

4
Mental Endurance and Strength

ALL THIS SOUNDS great, but what if you lose your passion along the way? I read a quote recently that suggested passions don't just exist on their own, but are built. So, to develop what you like into a passion, you need to see through it in the brightest and darkest days. You need to be resilient, and disciplined. I did not even like the sport of tennis for the first 3 years of playing it. Life throws many twists and turns, obstacles, and challenges at you every day. Nonetheless, it is that strength and passion in development that allows you to go and train even though you've had a personal relationship setback, or are forced to revisit your financial situation. It is that strength that allows you to overcome a bad mood, uncomfortable weather, or skipping on the live Super Bowl PPV because you have to train!

One solace, at least, is that working at your passion will lift your mood and spirit and alleviate the negative pain that you may be experiencing in your life. There is something about working towards a large life-long goal that calms you and refocuses you. The purpose gives you courage and strength, in the face of a difficult life. I've never felt happier than during my training days. Even the period of traveling and competition didn't give me as much joy as seeing myself progress and proving to myself the ability to stick to my own plans and follow my own path.

I realize people are different, and everyone gets motivated by different things, but all I can share here is my personal experience, and if you are anything like me, then I know you will benefit, and be happier as the result when following that long-term goal you set for yourself. Even if you are a senior adult player and set on the path of a 5-year plan, for example, I truly believe the quality of your life will improve if you are in sync with your passion.

5
Mental Strength In Matches

MOST OF THE mental issues experienced during a match are preventable with adequate preparation. If, for example, you get thirsty during a match, but you didn't bring a drink, then this physical issue could have been prevented with preparation. Mental health during a match is just as much dependent on preparation as your physical health.

How do you prepare mentally for a match? Visualization. What I recommend you do is spend some time before the match and explore all the different ways the match could go. Imagine that an inferior opponent beats you 6-0, 6-0 in front of your family and friends. Imagine you beating them 6-0, 6-0 with everyone you know watching. What kind of feelings would that bring up? Put yourself in these situations and explore your possible reactions. Now imagine the match is really close and you are battling for a third set after 2 tie-break sets. What mental state are you most likely to be in? What kind of steps would you take if you are not where you want to be?

Imagining all the possible scenarios a match can go will give you some insight of yourself and allow you to figure out ways to deal with the situation ahead of time. It's the same as preparing for that dehydration moment during the match. What would happen, for example, if you played with a vibration dampener (don't play with vibration dampeners), and lost your one and only during the match? Would you freak out, and blame the rest of the match on that event? How will you react if you break all the strings on your racquets, and you have to play with an unfamiliar one? Plan for such events, and you will notice how calmly you react to them when they happen, because in your mind, they have already happened.

> *"Your spiritual bearing must not be any different from normal. In normal times, and in times of combat, try to be no different."*

> —MM

Now that your homework is done, you need to focus on emotional stability. This does not mean 0 emotions. What emotional stability means is a lack of change in intensity or tone. You need to maintain the same emotional energy throughout the entire match. I describe it as trying to draw a painting on an even canvas vs. a bumpy, mountainous canvas. You give yourself a much better chance to perform if you eliminate emotional fluctuations as a variable. If you find yourself too sluggish or acting out, remind yourself of the energy level which allows you to perform best, and either pump yourself up, drink some caffeine, or take some deep breaths to calm down and refocus before your next point if you are too amped up. Internal methods of pumping yourself up and calming yourself down are more effective than the material ones I just mentioned. Though I cannot explain these methods, as only you can talk effectively your body's language. Take your time, and don't let individual events in the match phase you. You do this by planning your reactions ahead of time! Your opponent makes a bad call? Fine. You've planned your reaction ahead of time, and you're following through. Your shoe breaks? Fine. You've planned for this event, and it has 0 effect on your emotional stability. A helicopter flies by? Fine. You've planned what you're going to do, and how you will react—ahead of time!

Emotional change during a match can still happen even with extensive preparation. Dealing with this is the same as comforting a friend or a child. You need to sympathize with your emotional change and do your best to understand it. Once understood, it will subside. You must be that unmovable personality which your emotional self can align to. You must be steadfast when your mind wants to wonder. Just as in the learning process, this communication between you and your subconscious self is not verbal. The communication is done through feeling and observation. If you catch yourself internally or externally talking to yourself, then you are not communicating effectively. I also do not believe in the effectiveness of mantras. "I think I can; I think I can" will get you nowhere.

Some may tell you to do everything you can to empty your mind and let your body do what it's trained to do. This is all well and nice, but I believe you can do better than that (more on this later). Seek alignment and fluid communication with your mind, and team up with yourself to achieve a mutual goal. Convince yourself that victory and effective training is in yours and your subconscious mind's interests.

"Fright often occurs, caused by the unexpected."

—MM

Sometimes the reason for not performing at your highest potential is fear. Suppose you're mentally prepared to lose 6-0, 6-0 to that annoying player. You've visualized that possibility, and although not pleasant, you are going to be OK if it happens. However, point to point, and shot to shot, you still get tight when missing a certain shot over and over. After all of your training, such outcome is logically inconsistent and unexpected. Sometimes you know that you should go for that approach shot or a big drive, but you don't, because you've missed your last 3 in a row. So, instead of going for a 4th, you choose the "safe" shot and just get another weak ball back in play.

This is a very interesting situation which leads me to the "seen and unseen" in a tennis match. To alleviate that fear of making mistakes, you need to understand the dynamic and explain to yourself why going for the drive at that moment is better than pushing the ball back for just another groundstroke. This is just one example, but it can be applied to any shot that you are afraid of performing in a match. The seen effect is the immediate miss of your drive. The unseen is the pressure you could be adding to your opponent by making just 1 out of 4 shots. The unseen is the change in playstyle which this action may inspire in your opponent. The unseen is the options and possibilities that shots like these open for you and the influence on the outcome of the match.

I always tell people who are afraid to go for the right shot in tennis—the "stabbing in the alley" analogy. Although it may be graphic, it carries the point across. If you walked through an alley to get home from work for years, but one day someone stabs you and robs you while walking down that alley, will you walk down that alley again? What if you did, and you got stabbed a second time? This is how the human brain works. If we get burned just once or twice, we change behavior, and statistics don't matter. It doesn't matter you only got stabbed once out of 500 times walking down the same alley. You will still change your behavior. It's the same way with tennis shots. If someone gets really hurt just once or twice by your powerful drives (or whatever weapon you have for winning points), then they will think twice about floating balls to the service line against you. In effect, you are forcing them to raise their level of play, which results in more mistakes, as they can't play as effectively at a higher level. These mistakes add up and eventually, could cost them the match.

The "seen and the unseen" effect is powerful, and even if players are aware of it, it is still hard to fight nature's instinct and keep floating those balls to the service line—giving yourself 75% chance to win the point. Not only that, but you will improve your drive as you keep attempting them. Players need calibration, and if you only hit 3 shots, you don't really give your body a chance to calibrate. Instead of giving up on the shot you know is right, try to figure out and feel what you can do better to improve its success rate. If you don't do that, you are creating a weakness in your game. Be aware of these effects and give yourself courage through knowledge and understanding to do the right thing during a match or practice.

Always dictate the match. An analogy I often use for this is the "boats in the swimming pool." If you are in a boat in a swimming pool next to another person in their boat, when you rock your vessel back and forth, you create waves in the pool that the other person has to deal with. The waves will catch them off balance. Even though you are perhaps making more aggressive motions, you are not throwing yourself out of balance, because you are the one creating the waves and predict them with certainty. In such way, even though you are doing more in the match, and seemingly taking on more risk, you are dictating the flow of the match, and are in full control of what's happening. When you watch professional matches, try and notice this battle for control between the players, and how hard they work just to stay in control.

6
For The Parents

A PARENT'S ROLE is that of support. I haven't been a parent yet, but I've seen too many successful and unsuccessful parental practices, which gives me enough insight to comment on the topic.

As a tennis parent, your job is tough. You must be versatile, knowledgeable and cover the job of multiple professionals. You have to be the manager, physical trainer, coach, investor, psychiatrist, chemist, dietitian, life coach, driver, assistant, maybe even practice partner, and a few more roles. If you are wealthy and willing to invest much, then you are in a position to outsource many of these roles, but choose at least one or two, as your kid's inspiration will partly or fully be dependent on your enthusiasm for the sport and their progress. It's important to teach your kid about these roles, so they are at least aware of them, but it is not a good idea to make them perform these roles themselves as they are trying to focus on their practice. If the kid is to be great, then they need to be a master of one and not a jack of all trades. If you wanted to teach them how to be excellent managers, or drivers, or dietitians, then there are other books for that.

Kids draw and respond to the emotional energy from their parents. If you are a negative observer of their practice and matches and criticize mistakes and attitudes, then they will react accordingly with a nervous and angry behavior. They will pout and cry. They will blame others and you. They will cheat, lie, and complain. They will start to resent the sport, the whole experience and you.

If, on the other hand, the emotional energy of the parent is one of support, constructiveness, focus, and gratitude, then the kid will respond in kind and will play the role of that superstar in training that you envision them being.

If they make a big mistake—smile. It is not about winning or losing a specific point or match. It's about the overall direction of their development.

> *"If you defeat an enemy, [but] do so in a way contrary to what you have learned, you are not following the true way."*

> *—MM*

Is it worth sacrificing 3 months of training how to hit a drive, just to collect that tournament win by moonballing

100% of their shots? Will you be proud of their direction, or their character, or just their fitness and perseverance? It is your job to be that 3rd party observer that objectively guides their kid in what you know is the correct direction. The character you show to your kid is the character that they will most likely fall into and become. Winning by sacrificing principles is not really winning.

Kids are great at imitating their parents as it has been a major survival tactic throughout history. If you do what your parents do, there is a good chance you will survive and reproduce as they have. It's in us. So, knowing this, your behavior and the example you set for your child is much more important than what you tell them to do, or worse, what you yell at them for.

Do not try to be the player—they are the player. Your job is support and guidance, not force and micromanagement. If you are forcing an action, there is going to be blowback. Instead of force, try reasoning, and leading by example to inspire your child to do the right thing. Point out to them how you've learned from others in your field, and how it has helped you. This is what you are asking of them, is it not?

Be credible. If you are explaining to your kid a specific technique and you are not qualified to explain it, your kid will feel it and resent you and the comment. If you really believe in what you are telling your kid, then present your research, and explain why you believe what you are saying, then ask them for their opinion. After that, let the kid make their own decision on the matter. They are, and ultimately will be 100% responsible for their choices with their game, so teach them from the start—as soon as they are capable of reasoning.

Do not let your kid mistreat you, either. If you notice your kid develop a hostile unfounded response to you—talk about it, and resolve the issue. If there is a reason why your kid is mistreating you, then it needs to be addressed. If it's unfounded, then you need to let them understand the effect their actions have on you, and how it makes you feel. You will help develop empathy in your kid, and your relationship will be stronger and more productive. No kid wants to see their parents hurt, unless said parents have been hurtful to the kid before.

7
Lessons From The Tour

1. WALK ON sidewalks. It goes a little deeper than that. The lesson here is that you focus on your body's health and prioritize it over any fun and/or potentially harmful activity. There are more than a few instances where a tennis player in training will get hurt trying to play basketball for fun, or snowboarding, or doing some other random activity.

If you work in an office every day, then your livelihood is not endangered by a scratch or a pulled muscle. You can afford to be in a cast for a few months and be just as productive. If anything, it may help your sales when you have an easy story to tell. But if you are dependent on the perfect state of your body, then this becomes a big deal. Imagine you tell an office worker that by playing a video game, he has a 1% chance to lose 90% of his intelligence for 3 months or longer, which will render them useless at work and may cause them to be un-hirable for the rest of their lives. Would they do it? What if you called them a wuss? That's another thing you have to watch out for. Usually, tennis players in training are peer pressured into doing things that could set them back for months, if not forever. You are not a wuss! You are smart and courageous! It takes much more strength to decline than to be pressured into doing something.

Finally, the walking on the sidewalk comment refers to avoiding rough surfaces when walking from and to the tennis courts. "You never know; it could be something small that does it. You could fall in a small hole or trip on a rock. How stupid would you look then?"—CW (not exact quote)

2. Make conversation with everyone. This was a bit tough for me, but you will be surprised how much your connections help you through your efforts. You could be approaching the best trainer in the world's best friend, or family member. You could meet some nice people who offer you to stay the night for free. You could be talking to the future #1 in the world, or you could be talking to someone who quits tennis because you beat them so badly, but then goes on to become a successful financier and investor. This very investor may be what you desperately need 5 years down the road. What if you click with someone and you become training partners and/or doubles partners? Talk to people! I stumbled upon Brad Gilbert a few times in the stands, or before tournaments. Was it a useful conversation? No, but I did meet that Romanian coach who helped me win a match.

3. Don't excuse - adapt!

"[Don't] point fingers saying you ain't where you wanna be because of him, or her, or anybody. Cowards do that and that ain't you."

—*Sylvester Stallone as Rocky Balboa*

Every tournament is different. Whether you are playing on a fast indoor court or a sunny and humid clay court, you must adjust to the environment. Complaining how "bad you are on this surface" does you no good. You can mention out loud the conditions, but that's it. It's now time to deal with it. Modify your game if you must. The court is fast? OK, start counterpunching, driving, slicing, coming to the net, and doing flat serves. The court is slow? Ok, start playing with more topspin and find your rhythm. Also, get in better shape, as the match will be longer!

You should never use the referee as an excuse, or the bad calls of your opponent. Instead of blaming lost points in the match to things you can't control, adapt to them! Learn to expect and deal with the bad line calls. Don't even spend a second wallowing about how unfairly you think your match is going. I've always been fair to my opponents and give points away strategically. I'm not suggesting you do this, but it has helped motivate my opponents to be as fair as they can with their own calls. This example is meant to show you that there are things you can do to prevent, minimize, or eliminate obstacles like cheating opponents.

If you can't help what just happened, you can try to stop it from happening in the future.

I remember when I adopted this attitude of immediate adjustment. I was watching 2 very good tennis pros warm up a couple of days before a tournament. One of them said, "Wow, it's fast!" He was referring to the surface of the court. The lesson of the story is that these words were the only comment he made. Immediately after he spoke, there was nothing but the beginning of another rally. Neither of the players was phased by the fact that the surface was perhaps unfavorable—they started adapting right away. Complaining and blaming does not get you further, but action does.

4. Pay attention, review, and take notes. Be observant during a match. If you can afford it, have someone take notes on how you are winning or losing points. Get the statistics down and make notes on the causes of these statistics. Suppose your opponent had 30 winners during the match. That's all fine, but why? You need to know what is causing your opponent to have so much opportunity for winners. Is it that you are just slow? What about your shot quality? Perhaps your return is too short and weak. You need to know what is going right and wrong in the match to know exactly what you need to work on, and what you need to do more.

5. Learn and forget.

"Do not regret what you have done."

—MM

What I mean is, every mistake or strategy error must be respected and learned from, but you should not let the fact that you made an error drag you down. You need to practice a mindset that is consistent, and actively forget what just happened in order to approach the next point with an attitude that your body is used to. Also, you need to forget about what happened last time you played a specific opponent or where you were. You need to treat each match and each point as an individual event that has no ties to anything else besides the lessons you have already learned.

6. Give your strategy a chance to work. Sometimes the choices you make within a match work out in the short-term, but not in the long-term. Sometimes it's the opposite—you do something that costs you a few points but is very rewarding throughout the course of the match. You need to be tuned into the effects your shots and strategies are having, and what the likely outcome is as you persist. Usually, 2–3 games are not enough to really test the effects of your strategy.

7. Be informed. Call and confirm your time, date, and location of play. Speak to multiple people if you must, but do not get caught in a situation where you are misinformed. Understand your options. Read the rules and regulations of the ITF, ATP, WTA, USTA, or whatever organization you are playing under. Know what kind of clothing you can wear and what you can bring on the court. If you get caught uninformed, then not only will that cause you frustration, emotional imbalance, but it could also cost you the match. It's prudent to prepare ahead of time, and decide what your response is going to be as a certain regulatory challenge arises. Either be informed, or hire someone to be informed for you.

Being informed goes much deeper than just rules, regulation, and schedules. Being informed also means to know everything there is to know about the game of tennis. For example, you must know everything about playing tennis as a bigger frame person vs. smaller frame person. You need to know advantages and disadvantages of different brands of balls. You also need to know advantages and disadvantages of playing at high and low altitude, etc. Stay informed and knowledgeable! Keep up with the latest and newest trends and discoveries in the sport.

8. Be professional. Act as if tennis is your livelihood, because it is. Take the sport seriously, and if anyone asks you what you do for a living, you should tell them that you are a professional tennis player. This is not just important for your character development, but it will also test your ability to be honest and stick with your plans. Don't say things like "I'm traveling around and playing a bit." Because if you don't believe in what you are doing, the results will not be there.

Being professional goes even beyond your attitude; it means treating everyone else in a professional manner as well. It means knowing that there is money involved, and understanding the overall industry. You must understand that the lowest tier of tournaments lose money. They are sponsored by organizations to give people like you a chance. You are not entitled to play there and should feel privileged that you have the opportunity. If these organizations didn't exist, you'd be stuck playing 25 rounds of qualifying for a spot in the main draw of Wimbledon, unless they decide to go away with qualifying altogether and just do wild cards and invitations. Nobody owes you a spot in anything just because of your ranking, or how good your forehand looks.

Realize that the institutions, tournaments, and media are there only because they make enough money to sustain themselves financially by fans and viewers. Regardless of what your personal reasons are for being out there battling tennis balls, you must realize why everyone else is there too. Knowing this will help you maneuver through the professional world, and make things easier for you. Understand incentives.

8
Confidence

CONFIDENCE IS SOMETHING very sought after by not just tennis players, but virtually everyone who tries to excel at anything. "I just think I need more confidence!" It is a very common phrase I hear on the daily. What does that mean? What is confidence?

My belief is that confidence is roughly translated to certainty. How certain are you of the outcome of your actions? The more informed, experienced and trained you are in a specific action, the more aware you become of the possible outcomes. The more aware you are of what's going to happen, the more certain you are in your actions. This is confidence.

Confidence can be built up and squashed. Let's say you arrive at an outcome which you didn't expect. You are unprepared mentally, and your level of certainty (your confidence) may be crushed temporarily. If you, however, use this opportunity to add to your list of expected outcomes, then your confidence will increase in time. You can play with 100% confidence even if you know that there is a 95% chance of failure. The reason is that you are aware of the possible outcomes, and will not be surprised to see them play out. So, if you are asking how you can gain more confidence, you probably don't understand what it means. You probably are lacking sufficient experience, or have not been constructive with the experience you've gained. A confident player will not be shaken by any result—positive or negative. How confident are you?

9
Way Of The Void

THIS IS PERHAPS the most important part of my writing. I'm going to go totally Zen on you, so be prepared!

The biggest influence in my way of thinking and understanding the competitive mind has been an unlikely character—a 17th-century Samurai by the name of Miyamoto Musashi. I'm thankful that he made the wise decision to put some of his understanding of life and combat down in writing, so people like me and you can be enriched by their experience of not just their field, but life in general. His book of "Five Rings" (roughly translated) has been a lifesaver for me in my darkest times.

Personal story time! Between the ages of ~16 and 20 years of age, I was on the verge of depression, if not experiencing one. I was desperately looking for a reason to live. I'm sure some of you have gone through a similar stage and can relate. Fortunately for me, I found an inspiration which is very personal to me. I searched very deep within myself and asked what makes me happy and what makes me feel alive. This one condition was the zone. From then on, I sought after being in the zone.

You hear it all the time. "He is zoning!" or "She cannot be stopped!" Sports commentators and athletes talk about it all the time. I knew I experienced it for brief moments as well. It's that moment when everything around you seems to slow down, and you have complete control of yourself and the impact you make to your surroundings. It's the moment when it seems you really cannot make a calculative error in your movements. It's as if you are in a movie, and performing unbelievable feats.

To save my life, I thought, I had to pursue the zone. This turned out to be the wisest choice in my life. The next several years were a mix of training and reading, which could only be described as "pursuing the zone" or as Musashi describes it, roughly translated as the "void." Unfortunately, I stumbled upon this gem of writing very late in my pursuit, and so did not put what I was doing in the perspective I have now early in my career. Nevertheless, it gave me validation that I was on the right track, and now I'm an infinitely better person, competitor, and coach as a result. End of personal story!

What I will do is quote a very rough translation of the last chapter of his short book of Five Rings, and comment on what I believe he means and how I translate it to competition and tennis. If you are interested in reading the whole thing, I'm sure you can find it online for free and give it a read. It will take you about 45 minutes to read, but eternity to understand. I've read it at least 15 times so far, and I learn something new every time. One of my goals for this book is to have a similar effect on tennis players. I wish that they would take my writing one section at a time, ponder over it, try it out, and then move on to the next section. This way, my suggestions and principles can be instilled and have a deep impact on anyone looking to pursue this life of sport.

The book of the Void

> *"What is called spirit of the void is where there is nothing. It is not included in man's knowledge. Of course, the void is nothingness. By knowing things that exist, you can know that which does not exist. That is the void."*

In this first opening, Musashi is trying to explain in his own way what the zone (or void) is. He explains that the zone is not something that can be written in words and books, and then transferred from one person to another like a statistic, or a fact. It is not knowledge or a practical skill like knowing how to find an area of a circle or how to perform a forehand. It is intangible.

In the same short paragraph, he explains how to obtain the zone. It is obtained by the mastery and knowledge of all tangible things that do exist and are related to your field (or way). For example, you may experience the zone only once you have done so many forehands and backhands, that the body does them without even asking you for permission. It is the training of your subconscious mind. Once your movements become as instinctive as your breathing, then you will be able to truly observe them in peace, and be in the zone. It should come as no surprise that true mastery of a movement requires a very large number of repetitions, and that's a gross understatement. How many times have you taken a breath? That should put things into perspective!

> *"People in this world look at things mistakenly, and think that what they do not understand must be the void. This is not the true void. It is bewilderment."*

I believe what Musashi is referring to here is the common belief that to achieve peace in your mind, or the zone, one must empty their mind and think about nothing. This is false. The void is achieved through following a path and dedicating your life to it. It is achieved by doing, and not by inaction.

> *"In the way of the strategy, also, those who study as warriors think that whatever they cannot understand in their craft is the void. This is not the true void."*

Here he is reaffirming that people tend to mistake unclear cloudiness about a subject as the zone and pursue the mist itself. The zone is not achieved by pursuing empti-ness and eliminating clutter. It is not achieved by "clearing your mind from things," including real world events or emotions. It is, instead, achieved by observation, understanding, and action. It is achieved through certainty and experience.

> *"To attain the way of strategy as a warrior you must study fully other martial arts and not deviate even a little from the way of the warrior. With your spirit settled, accumulate practice day by day, and hour by hour."*

Here Musashi is emphasizing the importance of training, and how in your pursuit of the zone, you should not deviate from practice, as that is the path to the zone. He also suggests that we should learn all there is to learn related to our field (like physical training, diet, character, etc.). Stay informed, but stay on track.

> *"Polish the twofold spirit heart and mind, and sharpen the twofold gaze perception and sight."*

Interestingly, Musashi demonstrates here that he was aware of the mental duality. He was very aware of the subconscious mind, and the role it plays in physical performance. The heart and mind here are the conscious observer and the subconscious doer. By perception gaze, he means the analyzing mind, and by sight, he means the body actually viewing what is happening. In other words, master your thought, master your observation, and master their relationship.

> *"When your spirit is not in the least clouded, when the clouds of bewilderment clear away, there is the true void."*

What Musashi is saying here is that with enough practice, the body will start acting on its own with such certainty that the zone will be revealed to you. He also reiterates that the zone is not a product of doing things by not being aware. On the contrary, you attain the zone by being fully aware.

> *"Until you realize the true way, whether in Buddhism or in common sense, you may think that things are correct and in order. However, if we look at things objectively, from the viewpoint of laws of the world, we see various doctrines departing from the true way. Know well this spirit, and with forthrightness as the foundation and the true spirit as the way."*

I believe this wording means that it is best to trust ourselves and the pursuit of our goals above all. Many will try to sell us ideas that deviate from our path, but we must be resilient and trust our inner selves unconditionally.

"Enact strategy broadly, correctly, and openly. Then you will come to think of things in a wide sense and, taking the void as the way, you will see the way as void."

This sounds a bit like typical Japanese self-defining double talk, but let's break it down. I believe it means that if you search your field (or path—tennis, in our case) for the correct things to do, do the correct things without prejudice, and accept the void (the zone) as your pursuit, then your training, your competition, and all you do will result in the perception that your life is experienced as if you are in the zone.

This last sentencing is my favorite. I had to re-read it 20 times alone. I think the basic lesson here is that to achieve a life in the void, you must practice diligently in your field with a routine, have an open mind, and thus, you will come to interpret life as being in the zone.

Although not the greatest writer in the world (neither am I; we are athletes!), I believe everything Musashi says in this section to be potent, relevant, and true. I know this to be a fact, as I've experienced the zone much more frequently and for a longer period because of following his philosophy. These simple, but hard to understand words, have transformed my life and thought me not just how to be a great competitor and sportsman, but also how to approach life and its obstacles. I hope the same for you, if this is what you are after.

I'm going to leave you with another quote of his. It will be your challenge to translate and apply it to your tennis mentality.

> *"Generally speaking, the way of the warrior is resolute acceptance of death."*

The End.

If this book has taught you something, or you benefited in some way by reading it, you can help other potential readers by reviewing or referring these writings. I've made this an Amazon exclusive book, so a review on their site would be most helpful.
Thank You!

Made in the USA
Las Vegas, NV
15 May 2021

23046409R00066